About the Book

The profession of airline pilot is one of the most honored and rewarding in the world. It also is one of the most demanding. Few people need possess the high level of training, skill and dedication required of those who fly big, complex airplanes long distances through often-difficult weather conditions. In this interesting book, author Frank Stilley describes how you can become an airline pilot. He tells what training you need and what rewards and hard work you can expect in this profession that now is open to women as well as men. Numerous interviews with both men and women pilots give a fascinating inside view of what it means to be a pilot.

Here is Your Career

Airline Pilot

by Frank Stilley

G. P. Putnam's Sons • New York

Second Officer Claudia Jones makes a preflight check of a 727. (Continental Airlines)

Copyright © 1978 by Frank Stilley
All rights reserved.
Published simultaneously in Canada by
Longman Canada Limited, Toronto.
PRINTED IN THE UNITED STATES OF AMERICA
12216

Library of Congress Cataloging in Publication Data
Stilley, Frank.
Here is your career: airline pilot.
(Here is your career)   Includes index.
1. Aeronautics, commercial—vocational guidance—Juvenile literature. 2. Air pilots—Juvenile literature.
I. Title.
HD8039.A4S74   1978   629.132′52′023   78-9087
ISBN 0-399-20643-4

For Joy
A loving pilot of a happy marriage

Contents

1	Preparing for a Pilot Career	9
2	How to Learn to Fly	16
3	Learning to Fly the Military Way	32
4	Personal Traits That Help Make a Pilot	46
5	How Airlines Screen Prospective Pilots	52
6	Pilot Retraining by the Airlines	57
7	Here Come the Women—Again	66
8	The Silver-Winged Women	75
9	The Pilot's Pilot	87
10	The New Airliner Captain of Today	99
11	Flying Around the World	111
12	After Making Captain, What?	124
13	Takeoff to Tomorrow	132
	Index	143

Preparing for a Pilot Career

One of the most honored professions in the world today is that of the airline pilot. It also is one of the most demanding—and at the same time one of the most rewarding, financially and otherwise.

Few persons in this life are required to possess the high level of training, skill, personal qualification and dedication that typify the profession. If, in the mind of the general public, a certain amount of glamor and awe attaches to the airline pilot, it is well deserved by the commanding figure sitting at the controls.

The captain is in sole charge of one of the most complex machines ever devised by man and is responsible for the safety and comfort of 100 to 400 passengers as the giant craft hurtles through all manner of weather conditions. The pilot must know *everything* there is to know about his plane, from the workings of its many systems to countless procedures which can be employed in case of trouble.

To air travelers today, flying is quite routine. One boards

a plane with no qualms about getting to a destination, much in the manner of train passengers of yesteryear. Flying has become the safest travel mode of all—except perhaps for donkey cart on a dirt road in the country.

Two things have made this so. One is the exceptional advancement in technology of aircraft manufacturers. The other is the extraordinary skills possessed by pilots and cockpit crew. They didn't come by these skills easily. The tuition was years of study and work, often plus much personal expense and frustration.

But for every one who finally attains the goal, there are many who fall by the wayside somewhere along the route. It is not always because of lack of competence or aspiration. As of the present, and perhaps for some years to come, there are thousands of extremely qualified pilots who can't get a job with a major airline. Even with continued expansion of the airline business there just aren't that many pilot spots available.

Offhand it might seem that the prospects of eventually getting to be a pilot border on the hopeless. That, happily, is not necessarily the case. Much depends on the individual, as always. For the young man *or* woman who has any thought of seeking to become an airline pilot of the future, the thing to do is make up your mind and stick to your resolve. Do it *now*. And the younger you are the better it will be—for you. Age 16 or younger isn't too early.

There are numerous things you can do to start preparing yourself. We'll discuss them later. Every single one of them will stand you in good stead.

But first, there are some most important things that the

Flight instruction in a 747 cockpit simulator. The runway view is a television projection, and through computerization varies precisely as it would in actual operation of aircraft controls. (American Airlines)

fledgling must know before making a final commitment.

One is that you must be in good—in fact, perfect—health. You must keep yourself that way. Airlines will accept no less.

You must not be a user of drugs or narcotics—not even of occasional marijuana.

Further, on the subject of health, you must have perfect eyesight. Vision corrected by eyeglasses or contact lenses is not acceptable.

You must get a college education. This has become a prime requirement with most major airlines. It is not a critical matter as to what subject you choose for your major course. However, you'll probably have an extra advantage if you do some or most of your college work in physics, mechanics, math or similar technical courses.

It also will help the pilot candidate to have a pleasing personality and an equable disposition.

Other desirable attributes are above-average intelligence, an ability to think clearly and quickly, an analytical mind and reasonably good manual dexterity.

One other attribute perhaps is as important as all the others combined: an unflagging determination. That one, of course, is an immense asset no matter what one does in life.

From a realistic standpoint there are two, and only two, ways to prepare for an ultimate career as an airline pilot.

One could be called the civilian route. That is, you learn to fly on simple, small planes by taking flying lessons at a local airport. Once the student obtains a pilot's license, he or she continues to study and train on progressively larger planes, through multiengine propeller-driven craft to small-

PREPARING FOR A PILOT CAREER

er and then larger jets. This program can be very expensive and require many years. It also can be difficult to gain enough experience on large jets to meet application requirements of major airlines.

The big airlines do not accept persons who have not flown before and train them from the ground up. They want only applicants who already are highly experienced. Generally, these pilots must have at least 1,000 hours of flying time in multiengine aircraft. Even after acceptance they are put through a rugged retraining course by the airline itself.

Still, the young person who sets out to pursue a pilot career by way of the civilian route is not faced by insurmountable obstacles. He or she can work at other jobs while learning to fly or taking advanced training. Then very often pilot jobs can be obtained on smaller commercial craft as training progresses. Each new pilot-level attained provides opportunity for employment on still larger planes.

In time the young pilot may be flying for small feeder passenger airlines, freight lines or perhaps even corporate piston planes or jets. The more one advances, the more one qualifies to fly increasingly sophisticated craft, with a corresponding increase in pay. Some persons, in time, have been able to get flying jobs abroad on much larger planes than in the United States.

In any case, as so often happens in other pursuits, one thing has a way of leading to another for the person with overwhelming desire and dogged determination.

The second way to the captain's seat of a jetliner is by way of military service. In many ways this is much to be preferred.

Any young person who has the personal qualifications

listed above and is accepted for training by the Air Force, will get the finest flight training in the world. Moreover, it will take less than a year to prepare the newcomer to fly a twin-engine supersonic jet. Thereafter, the pilot may get training on huge military jets comparable to the civilian airliners of today.

With the Air Force, the trainee starts from scratch. It doesn't make any difference whether the trainee has had any flying experience or not. He must have a college education, however.

Air Force training is intense, and commercial airlines regard it highly. The student works at it virtually night and day for 49 weeks, with little time for anything else except eating and sleeping. There is no other comparable course for the beginner anywhere. Standards are extremely high.

Once the undergraduate training is completed, the pilot is currently committed to remain in the Air Force for 5 years. During that period the pilot will develop the maturity to command the most advanced aircraft the nation possesses.

That is why most of the pilots flying commercial jetliners today got their training in military service. The total ranges up to 80 or 85 percent on the major airlines.

From the beginning of the airline industry in the 1930s until quite recently, the profession of airline pilot was strictly a male preserve.

Now, however, women are beginning to get a chance to show their ability, both in civilian and military aviation. As of late 1977 about two dozen women had been accepted by major airlines and, after company training, qualified to fly passenger jets.

However, most were serving as second officers—in effect, as flight engineers. They were biding their time, awaiting openings to advance to the rank of first officer, or copilot, and eventually the captain's seat.

At the same time the Air Force had a small number of women in training. This was largely a test program to ascertain what specific functions would be most appropriate for use of their skills. Women are forbidden by law to fly in combat, but the Air Force does have many support missions which women pilots could fly.

Women have been waiting a long time for their chance. Now they're on their way at last. Airlines expect they will have far more female pilots in future years.

2

How to Learn to Fly

Many of the veteran pilots flying jetliners today got their first taste of flying by hanging around small-town airports as youngsters.

They did menial jobs: washed planes, fueled them, helped mechanics, pushed planes in and out of hangars, even swept out hangars and offices. They did anything they could to be around planes and talk to people who flew them. Sometimes they got paid a little, and often they didn't earn anything.

In other spare time they studied everything they could about planes—how they are put together, what makes them fly and how you fly them. They learned what you do in different kinds of weather and what you don't do.

In time their enthusiasm got them flights with people who owned the planes or with people who gave flying lessons. Occasionally they would be allowed to take the controls to learn how a plane handled in flight. Some learned from their fathers, mostly old barnstormers, when they were barely big enough to see out of the cockpit. Many actually became pilots before they were old enough to get a license.

From that kind of a beginning they progressed to larger and better planes. You may ride with some of them these days on 727s, 707s, DC-10s or 747s.

Pilots say it is still possible for a youngster to do pretty much the same thing today, particularly around small airports.

But for those who can't, it is quite easy and much less time-consuming to take flying lessons. Nearly every airport of any size has a flight instruction school. Even around the smallest there probably will be someone authorized to give flying lessons. The cost varies, but is not unduly expensive.

There are two types of flying schools, generally speaking. One kind is approved by the Federal Aviation Administration (FAA); the other is not. In the former, the course will include much more instruction in the basics of aviation. The course also will require less time, because it is in a more concentrated form.

Whether you choose either the civilian or military flight path to your ultimate destination as an airliner captain, the flying school is a good way to begin. While you don't necessarily need previous flight experience as far as the Air Force is concerned, it will make training there much easier. You'll already know what flying is like, the basics will be familiar and the wear and tear on your nervous system will be vastly reduced.

You must be at least 16 years old to get a private flying license. To do that you must have been able to perform a solo flight under approval of an authorized instructor.

The cockpit of a 747. At right is the flight engineer's control panel. There probably are more than 1,000 instruments and controls in the cockpit. (American Airlines)

With a private license you may fly yourself, your parents, your friends or others, but the trip must be for pleasure and not for hire. You also must fly only under visual flight rules. That means you must be able to see the ground at all times.

A list of FAA-approved flight training schools may be obtained by writing the Department of Transportation, Federal Aviation Administration, Washington, D.C. 20591.

The department also furnishes information on schools providing FAA-approved instruction in flight-related skills which require government certification. These skills are those of flight dispatchers, airline maintenance inspectors, airframe and engine mechanics, instrument technicians and radio technicians.

Before going any further, it probably should be said that *almost anyone can be taught to fly.*

The chief ingredient for those who think they'd like to make a profession of it is desire.

What is it like to learn to fly? Larry Strain of American Airlines is amply qualified to describe the process. He was one of those who began learning at the age of about 13— sitting next to his father, one of those aforementioned old barnstormers, years ago in what was called a Stinson "station wagon."

He had soloed around 16, before he even got a student training license. Since then he has flown almost every kind of plane up to and including the 747. He also has a sailplane pilot's license.

Larry describes the type of training a student receives at an FAA-approved school.

You start with work in ground school, which is much like that of study in elementary or high school—"the chalk and blackboard routine." Later you begin flying with an instructor.

Through these combined programs you learn the basics of flight: what supports an aircraft in flight—thrust over drag, lift over gravity—what turns the airplane, and so on.

You learn what the airplane will do and what it won't do; what will cause the plane to fall.

You're taught airspeed reference numbers, and that you must maintain a speed at or above this number or else the plane is going to stall. Stalling means that the craft is losing airflow over the wings and no longer can support flight. The ultimate result is that you begin to fall out of the sky.

You learn to recover from that by pushing the plane's nose over to regain the airspeed you have lost. With the control stick you push the down-elevator. That's because if you have a full up-elevator, you keep the plane in a flat flying attitude and it cannot gain speed. It will just drop, flatly. When you push the nose over it's like going downhill in a car. You pick up speed. Once you've picked up the necessary speed you can continue your flight.

All these things you practice, and also such things as the angle of bank on the airplane. In other words, how much you dip the wing to make a turn. Turning has a relationship to the airspeed at which the plane will stall.

While flying straight and level you can sustain speed at, say, 100 miles an hour. As you increase the bank of the aircraft, or the tilt of the wings, the stalling speed increases because you are not in the flat, level, horizontal attitude

Giant terrain model which provides the view through cockpit simulator windows for airline pilot trainees. Television camera in background (center right) is moving along an "airport" runway. (American Airlines)

which the plane's wing was basically designed to be in. Thus the speed at which you will lose flying ability, or reach the stalling-out point, is increased.

After you've learned the basics in ground school you're taken up by an instructor. You begin putting into practice what you learned on the ground. First you do basic maneuvers, such as straight and level flight and gentle turns.

On your first takeoff and landing you will follow the instructor through the procedures. You will just be on the dual controls feeling the forces that are required to raise the nose to a takeoff attitude. On landing you'll feel the cushion effect of the air as you approach the runway, and learn how much you can depend on the downflow of air off the wings to help you approach the ground.

For the next several hours of flying with the instructor you will practice these things. The number of hours will depend on your proficiency as a student.

But finally one day the instructor will say, "Okay, kid, you're ready." You'll taxi up to the hangar and he'll step out and say, "It's yours. I want you to make a takeoff and come around and land and taxi back up here." Your real shakeout moment has arrived.

Says Larry Strain, "That's probably one of the most thrilling moments that a flier can have, because now you are pitted against the elements . . . the machine and the elements. Oddly enough, I think probably one of the best landings I ever made was when I soloed, because the adrenalin was really flowing.

"You know that once you get up there, there is no recourse other than to put into practice what you've learned. There is no one to turn to and say, 'I need help—can you help me,' other than by radio. There's no one there to caution you about too steep a bank or too flat an approach angle.

"It's a thrilling moment."

Tradition has it that after you land, either your shirttail or your tie is cut off by your instructor. That symbolizes that you have soloed. You are now authorized to go out and fly the airplane by yourself.

In a way, that's only the beginning.

Instruction at an FAA-approved school requires a minimum total of 40 hours of dual and solo flying time. As the student moves into more complex aspects of flying after soloing, he or she will receive training in such matters as weather interpretation, cross-country flying, radio navigation, coping with unusual airplane attitudes and phases of instrument flying. However, the work with instruments will not be sufficient to gain the student an instrument "ticket," a higher-grade license permitting instrument flying when visual rules cannot be followed because of weather conditions.

The advanced training after soloing will consist of more practice landings and takeoffs, crosswind landings, stalls, turns around specific ground points such as highway intersections and other maneuvers.

In due time, after some further ground instruction, will come a first cross-country flight. It may be 15 or 20 miles.

The purpose is for you to learn that the charts you have will adequately depict what is on the ground. You'll fly over a big highway that a railroad crosses and the instructor will ask, "Do you see it on the map? Do you see the refinery over

AIRLINE PILOT

there that's also shown on the map? Okay, where are you in relation to those?" You then point out your position on the map.

Before long there will be much longer cross-country trips. These will be more critical because you must now start figuring such things as fuel flow, elapsed time, speed and the time necessary to reach the next point you're supposed to reach.

"These become very critical in flight," explains Larry Strain, "not only as a student pilot but in today's big jets too . . . the fuel that you have remaining, how long you can hold if you have bad weather. It's really basics that you can apply later on in flying. All these things come into play."

One fine day the instructor will say, "I want you to go take the written test." He means the FAA's test. He'll give you a note to the FAA saying you're ready. So you present yourself at the nearest FAA office and sit down with your little "computer" to take the written examination. It will cover all the things you've learned, or should have. The little "computer" you'll use actually is a sort of round slide rule enabling you to compute speeds, fuel consumption, elapsed time and time remaining on theoretical flights.

For the next ten days to two weeks you'll probably sit around biting your nails, waiting to learn whether you passed. The day you receive notification by mail that you did will be a glorious one. You'll probably rush out to find your instructor, exploding with pride over your wondrous achievement.

But that's still not the end of the story.

* * *

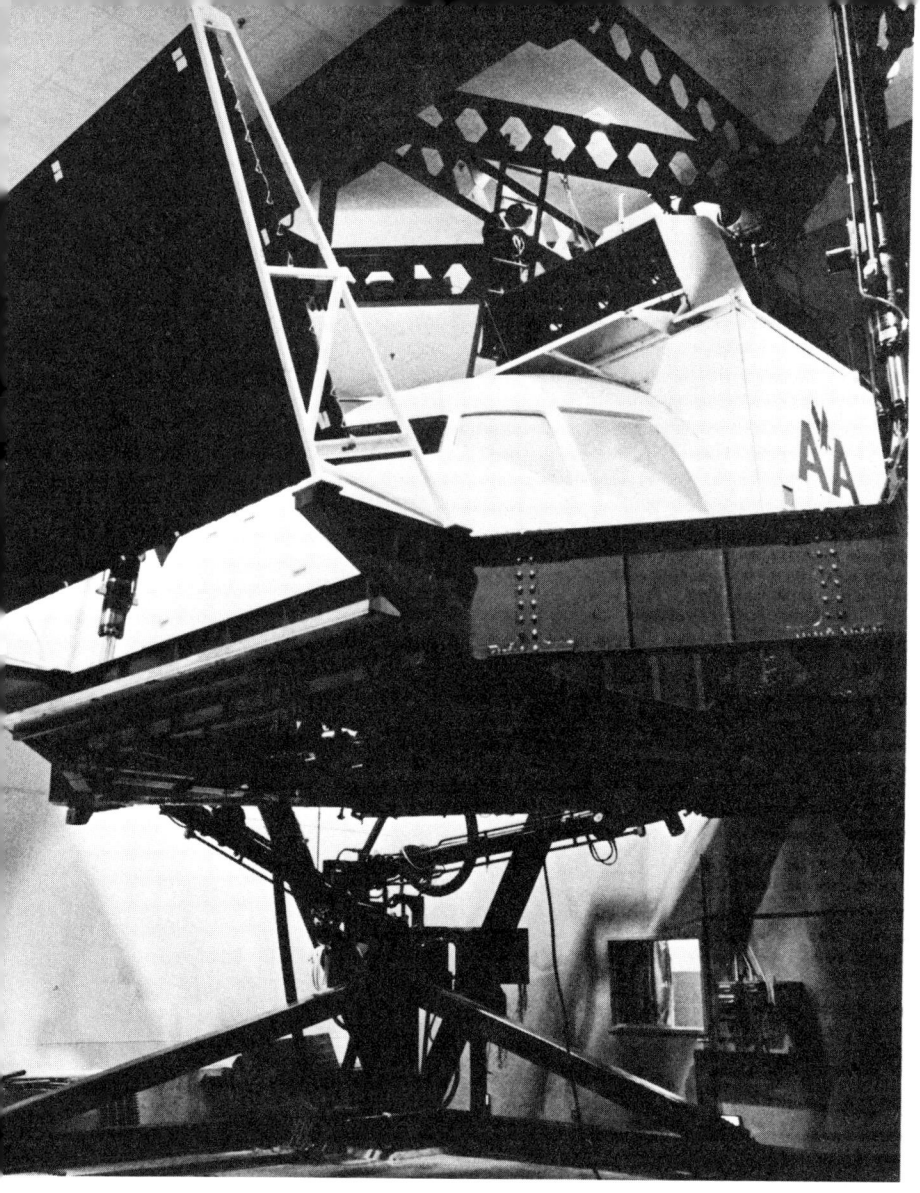

Hydraulic mechanisms under cockpit simulator create aircraft motion effects of all types. Other devices duplicate sounds. At upper left is screen on which "flight" views are seen from cockpit. (American Airlines)

Now you're going to get the works, and truly so, from your instructor. This will be a warm-up for what you'll get later.

The instructor will put you through all the paces over and over again, from preflight plane checks to every flight maneuver in the books. He'll play the devil's advocate to a fare-you-well. He wants to be absolutely certain that you're ready for the checkout that really counts.

It won't be long until one day at the airport your instructor will say, "I'd like to introduce you to Mr. so-and-so from the FAA. Today is *the day.*"

Thereupon you'll "preflight" your plane just as a captain or other flight officer does with every jetliner before every flight today.

You'll walk around the plane making a visual inspection. You'll look in the fuel tanks and at the oil dipstick, check air pressure in the tires, look for any damage to the plane's skin. Once you're satisfied that everything is right, you'll get in the plane with the FAA inspector.

Meanwhile, he will have been asking all manner of questions. What was the tire pressure on the main landing gear? How many gallons of fuel were in the tank by your visual observation? How far can this airplane fly? And on, and on. The FAA inspector wants to satisfy himself that you're fully versant with the performance of the plane.

Once in the cockpit you'll go through a before-start-engine checklist. Every type of plane has a certain number of things to be done or checked before revving up. On a big airliner the list is quite extensive, as you doubtless suspect.

After starting the engine, checks must be made to make certain of proper oil pressure and temperature, and to verify that the engine's RPM counters are working. The radios are turned on, and then used to get information from the airport on wind and barometric pressure. Settings are made on appropriate cockpit instruments.

A call is then made to ground control for taxi-out instructions. Once given, they are acknowledged by you and the plane is then taxied out to the end of the runway to be used.

There you run up the engine to see if it is working properly and make sure that all flight controls and surfaces are free and operating. If so, you're ready for takeoff.

You radio the tower again: "Tulsa tower, Cessna 21 Delta, ready for takeoff, 35-right [the runway designation]."

Tower: "Cessna 21 Delta, cleared for takeoff, 35-right."

Runways are numbered by compass headings. Thus 35 means 350 degrees on the compass, 9 is 90 degrees and 1 is 10 degrees. At many airports there are parallel runways. This accounts for the right and left designations.

Off you go—with an eagle eye on you.

The inspectors who check out beginning pilots are very professional whether they are actual FAA employes or people assigned to act in behalf of the FAA. So many people are learning to fly nowadays that the FAA often designates certain flight instructors to do checkout work.

In working with you they'll be likely to chat about a lot of things in friendly fashion so as to make you feel more comfortable. They know that you're probably nervous, just as you would be if you were taking some other important test, such as a bar examination to practice law. They'll do their best to make you feel at ease.

AIRLINE PILOT

They will not be trying to trick you in asking questions about flying. They'll only be testing your knowledge and skills learned in training.

Once the two of you are in the plane and ready to go, the inspector will probably say something like "Let's go out and make a normal takeoff and depart the area, then we'll do some high work."

By "high work" he means that you're going to climb to a safe altitude where you can demonstrate such things as stalls. This is where you pull the throttle back and bring the nose of the airplane up to let the aircraft drop below its flying speed. Then you'll show how to recover from the stall and maintain flying attitude once more.

The inspector will have you work some radio navigation problems. One way of doing this is tuning in an aviation radio station operated by the FAA and then heading your plane toward it.

Thereafter you will be directed to perform many maneuvers. Among them will be 360-degree turns and perhaps "eights." The latter are figure-eight turns around some fixed point on the ground, such as an intersection of two roads or a bridge over a river.

The instructor may reach up and pull the throttle off, saying "Okay, you've just lost your engine. Show me where we're going to make an emergency landing."

You'll have to spiral down, set up an emergency landing approach to whatever spot appears best under the circumstances. It could be a cornfield or a road. Once the instructor sees that you can make it he'll let you restore power and regain altitude.

The normal flight check will last about an hour, and it is

much like taking an automobile driving test. The instructor will be sitting in the right-hand seat with a clipboard, making notes all the while. He will never offer any remarks such as "very good" or "very bad." There will be only straight instructions as to what you are to do.

On return to the airport he may try you out on a "go-around." As you make the approach and prepare to land, the inspector will suddenly say that there's a car or other obstruction on the runway, so abort the landing. You'll have to apply power, pull up and continue flight. This is to check out your reflexes in case of such an emergency.

After landing, the inspector also could have you start another takeoff and then cut your engine, as might happen if you unexpectedly lost engine power on a takeoff. The inspector wants to see how you handle that.

Many things will run through your mind while you're taking your flight test. "I wonder how I did on that?" you'll ask yourself often.

Every time you know that some specific maneuver was not done to the best of your ability (and you will know), you'll sense the tension in your body and worry whether you're passing the all-important test.

All in all, your checkout flight is nothing more than a practical test to determine if you've learned your lessons well and are capable of handling a plane properly in all circumstances.

Almost all beginning pilots will experience increasing anxiety as the examination nears its end because the inspector won't have given you any indication of whether you've passed or failed.

Some of the most pleasing words you may ever hear in

your life could come when you've landed, taxied up to the ramp and shut down the engine and the inspector says something akin to "Well, let's get our stuff together and I'll go in and write you out a ticket."

This means a temporary airman's certificate. The inspector will type it out and issue it to you on the spot.

You will now be a full-fledged private pilot.

You now can show off your exciting new skills by taking anybody you wish for a ride—your spouse, children, relatives, friends—as long as you don't do it for pay.

In about six weeks you will get a permanent airman's certificate from the FAA aeronautical records center in Oklahoma City.

But what if you don't pass the test?

You'll get another chance after further practice to eliminate your shortcomings. The inspector might say, for example, "Look, your landings and takeoffs were fine but you need to work on your stall recoveries, so let's go talk to your flight instructor."

Or he might say to the instructor, "Everything was fine except that I wasn't completely satisfied with his work under the hood."

At some point during the check flight a hood will be put over your eyes in such a way that you must fly on instruments. That is to demonstrate the capability in case you should sometime get caught in freak weather conditions and weren't able to navigate visually.

Technically it is illegal for a pilot to fly by instruments unless he or she has an instrument rating certificate. But a private pilot must know how to do it in case of emergency.

"Give him two more hours of instrument work and I'll recheck him on that phase only," your flight instructor would be told by the FAA man.

That done, the instructor would make an appointment with the FAA inspector for a follow-up check flight.

Chances are, you'll be a real whiz at instrument flying by then.

3

Learning to Fly the Military Way

With justifiable reason, the United States Air Force maintains it trains pilots better and faster than anybody in the world.

In just 49 weeks a young person who never even saw the inside of a plane before can be flying a supersonic jet. A short while after that the new pilot will be flying huge bombers, tankers or cargo planes.

The Air Force doesn't hesitate to remind people, either, that its pilots were the ones who took our spacecraft to the moon.

Commercial airline people hold Air Force fliers in the very highest regard. That's the reason why so many of them are hired by airlines after leaving military service. They are highly trained professionals and today's airliners are very much like the planes they flew in service. In some cases they are the very same.

Gaining acceptance for what the Air Force calls Undergraduate Pilot Training is no snap. The service has far more

LEARNING TO FLY THE MILITARY WAY

applicants than it can accept. In recent years about 700 have been selected for training annually.

But for young men and women who think they'd like to try the Air Force, the criteria are that you must:

—Be between 20½ and 26½ years of age.

—Have a college degree.

—Pass a rigid physical examination. In fact, you must be in perfect health.

—Pass the Air Force officers' qualifying test. The test takes about 8 hours. The first half is an examination for basic knowledge and intelligence. The second relates to mechanical aptitude and dexterity in areas relating to pilot activity and navigation.

Upon passing the officers' qualifying test, the student goes to officers' training school for 90 days. With graduation from this school the trainee becomes a second lieutenant. All Air Force pilot trainees must be commissioned officers.

There are several other routes for obtaining an officers' commission and entering Undergraduate Pilot Training. College graduates who have served in the Air Force Reserve Officers' Training Corps are eligible, since they hold the rank of second lieutenant on graduation. So are graduates of the Air Force Academy, whether or not they have taken any flight training at the academy. Additionally, officers already serving in the Air Force may apply for pilot training.

There are five Air Training Command bases where undergraduate flight training is given. They are Williams Air Force Base in Arizona, Columbus Air Force Base in Mississippi, Vance Air Force Base in Oklahoma, and the Laughlin and Reese Air Force bases in Texas. These bases are used because they have good flying weather most of the year.

The entire training course is conducted at one base. This is done to eliminate unnecessary student moves and reduce training costs. Just incidentally, the Air Force estimated in 1977 that the training cost per student was $238,700.

The 49-week course involves approximately 800 hours of actual study and flying. This total includes about 500 hours in ground training, 70 hours or so in simulators which duplicate cockpits and actual flight, and some 210 hours of flying. The total does not include a good many student hours devoted to proverbial "midnight oil" activity. Also not counted are the hours spent in preflight and postflight briefings by instructors.

The upshot is that aviation study is a full-time business for the student. Says an Air Force officer, "You study the night before for your work the next day. But, unlike college where you may read a book once and hope to get by, in training you will read it several times. You must *know* it and you must *demonstrate* that you know it. There's no way of fudging."

A typical day of pilot training as the student progresses, says the officer, is something like this:

In the morning you go to classes. They could be on such subjects as navigation, weather, engine performance, aerodynamics and airframe construction.

In the afternoon you go on the flight line. There you sit down with an instructor and go over the mission planned: what you intend to do from takeoff to landing, what the instructor expects you to do and how you intend to do it.

You fly the mission and on return discuss everything about it with the instructor: what you did right and what you

The first women ever to be trained as military pilots by the United States Air Force line up in front of a T-38 Talon training aircraft. (U.S. Air Force)

AIRLINE PILOT

did wrong, and how to do it the next time. After your evening meal you study textbooks for the class next morning.

This study covers not only the scheduled classwork but also a book on the particular plane you're flying.

"Modern jet aircraft are very complicated. Each one has its own operating instructions and technical manual, some of which may be as much as six inches thick," according to the Air Force spokesman.

"In undergraduate training the manuals are only one to two inches thick, but they are a student's bibles. A pilot must know everything that's in them. Some of it, which we call emergency procedures, you must know verbatim—you recite word for word—and are able to respond instantly."

First jet flight training is conducted in the T-37, a twin-engine subsonic jet. It is described as a fast and rugged aircraft equal in speed and maneuverability to most fighter planes of World War II.

With his instructor seated at his side in the T-37, the trainee makes practice flights of about 80 minutes in a specific area. During these the student learns the characteristics of the craft, takeoff and landing techniques, emergency procedures, aerobatics, navigation, cross-country flying and night, instrument and formation flying.

Once the T-37 is mastered, the student transfers to the T-38 Talon for 120 hours of training. The T-38 is the Air Force's first supersonic undergraduate pilot training aircraft. With its twin jet engines the Talon is capable of achieving speeds over 800 mph (Mach 1.2) and flying at an altitude of more than 50,000 feet. The Air Force regards the T-38 as an excellent craft for preparing pilots for transition to higher-speed operational planes.

During flight in the Talon the trainee will spend approximately 46 hours operating under visual flight rules, 22 hours flying by instruments and 45 hours in formation flight.

The service figures that the student puts in a 12-hour work day on the average. This will include classwork, physical training, operating a simulator and evening study, in addition to actual flying.

Academic training includes navigation, flight planning, weather, aerospace physiology, aircraft systems operation, aircraft accident prevention, principles of flight, applied aerodynamics, flight instruments and instrument procedures.

Military training subjects cover such things as personal and professional conduct as an officer, physical training and moral leadership.

Flying instructors are specially selected military pilots and graduates of the Air Force Pilot Instructor Training School at Randolph Air Force Base in Texas. They must meet rigid personal, flying and professional standards.

Each one is normally assigned two or three students. The Air Force says the instructor is "basically a teacher who must have patience, a keen understanding of human nature and an eye for painstaking detail."

Additionally, "the instructor is supplied with some of the most modern and effective teaching aids. One of the more recent is a computer which stores each student's record of training activities. This provides the instructor with access to all training information on each of his students. Those who are experiencing difficulty in any portion of flying can be identified early and corrective action taken promptly."

When the student completes the undergraduate course he'll have a pair of silver wings ceremoniously pinned on his uniform. He's now an Air Force pilot—and ready for bigger and better things in the way of aircraft.

Usually the new pilot goes into training for the particular aircraft he will fly permanently. It might be a jet fighter or bomber or tanker or cargo craft. The training may take several months.

Afterward the pilot could be assigned to many different bases around the world. But, as was mentioned earlier, the pilot is obligated to remain with the Air Force at least five years.

Many who eventually leave, for airline or other civilian aviation jobs, remain in the Air Force Reserve. They devote a certain amount of time each year to maintaining their proficiency with military aircraft and other military activities, and receive pay for this duty.

When the new pilot proceeds to training on larger or more sophisticated planes, he will in effect be starting all over again.

He must begin anew with ground school to learn everything there is to know about the plane he will be flying—and how flying it will be different from previous craft. He'll learn, for instance, that a B-52 bomber is handled in a vastly different fashion than a T-38.

For a while he'll be flying as copilot, but in time he'll become an aircraft commander himself.

The T-37 in top photo is the first jet to be flown by Air Force trainees. Students then progress to the T-38 Talon supersonic jet, shown below. (U.S. Air Force)

AIRLINE PILOT

* * *

A young person entering Air Force pilot training need not have flown before. But there are distinct advantages in having done so.

One is the fact that the trainee has no initial fear of flying, won't be upset when hit by G-, or gravity, forces for the first time and will be less troubled by rough weather.

The introduction to G-forces can be dismaying and in some cases critical to a flying career. There are a few individuals who simply cannot tolerate the crushing effect on the physical system. These people are "washed out," as the saying goes—not permitted to continue training.

In the flight training a person must be able to withstand more than seven times the normal force of gravity. On the T-38 it will occasionally reach seven plus Gs. However, in most cases the body becomes acclimated to it.

Some trainees fail for other reasons. Physical problems may develop, such as ulcers. Occasionally a student will discover that, after learning to fly at 100 knots, it isn't possible to cope with the stress of flying at 500 knots or more. Some will find that they just don't have the temperament for flying, or the desire they thought they did.

The Air Force has found that in a class of 700 about 11 percent will fail or leave for one reason or another.

There are a few cases in which the Air Force makes an allowance for a physical change in the student after training has begun. For example, a student must have 20-20 vision at the outset, but less perfect vision sometimes develops and will be accepted.

"The reason is that once the Air Force has a good deal of

LEARNING TO FLY THE MILITARY WAY

money invested in your training, it becomes a matter of sound business management versus minor physical defects which do not affect a pilot's efficiency," says an Air Force pilot.

While veteran airmen are generally agreed that almost anybody can be taught to fly if given enough time, the key to Air Force training is the time factor. The service wants people who are capable of learning, and learning well, in the time it deems sufficient.

That doesn't mean that one must be perfect every step of the way. Students are given further chances if they should fail in some aspect of the training. However, repeated failures will lead to questioning before a board of officers. The student must then have a very convincing explanation of his failures if he is to remain in training.

Even if washed out as a pilot, the student still may elect to become a navigator.

One thing the Air Force will not tolerate in the least is experimentation with drugs, either before or after entering service. Even after becoming a pilot, it is said, anyone found to have smoked a single marijuana cigarette could be grounded for a year.

For the young person bent on preparing for an airline pilot's job through military training, the Air Force offers almost the only opportunity today and certainly by far the best one.

The Army and Navy no longer fly the great variety of planes they once did. For all practical purposes, the Army doesn't have airplane pilots. It has helicopter pilots.

AIRLINE PILOT

Helicopter training does not qualify the pilot to fly an airplane, even though the helicopter might be jet-driven.

The Navy operates only a few multiengine jets, mainly Hercules turboprop C-130s. The turboprop is considered a jet, since its propellers are driven by jet engines.

The Air Force trains pilots so that they can fly any type of airplane—those with reciprocating (or piston) engines, turboprop craft or jets. In the Navy the training is either as a prop-plane or jet pilot. The pilot must remain with the type of plane on which training has been received.

Some people in aviation have at times expressed the view that jet fighter pilots eventually make the best airline pilots, possibly because of their training to think and act quickly.

The Air Force spokesman is quick to take issue with this notion.

"It's like saying racing car drivers make the best automobile drivers. Or that people who drive motorboats are the best sailors."

Another thing in which the Air Force takes pride is the uniformity of skill which its pilots attain. In a special study, it found that pilots came out of undergraduate training with somewhat different degrees of proficiency, but that after two years in the service their skills were about the same.

Whether airlines can continue to depend on military trainees for their future stockpile of pilots is a question.

The Air Force, for instance, was in 1977 only about half its size of previous years, with the number of pilot trainees reduced as well. Obviously, however, it must continue to train pilots to replace those who leave service, become physically disabled, retire because of age or die. The

Captain Connie J. Engel (right) and First Lieutenant Sandra M. Scott inspect the nose gear of a Northrup T-38 Talon, one of the aircraft in which they will be training to become Air Force Pilots. (U.S. Air Force)

number of trainees at any given time will depend on the world situation.

Should it remain low for years to come, it is possible that airlines may have to set up training facilities of their own, perhaps jointly.

Young women's prospects for Air Force training are growing much brighter, though the numbers that may be accepted for pilot training remain to be determined. Heretofore, regulations shut them out completely.

On September 2, 1977, the first class of 10 young women was graduated from the undergraduate pilot training course. Another class was in training, and announcement had been made that applicants would be accepted for a third.

This training is in the nature of a test program for the Air Force to determine how best women could be employed as pilots. Since they are precluded by law from flying combat planes, their role naturally would be limited to other types of craft.

The Air Force has several categories of flight work in which women could be utilized. These include cargo, passenger and other support planes as well as training aircraft. Two of the first 10 women pilots were becoming flight instructors, and thus would be teaching men to fly.

In any case, the Pentagon has recently come under heavy pressure to accept many more women in all military services and has announced plans to do so—though not yet as many as some outside groups have demanded.

Women already have been permitted equal opportunity to enter the Air Force Academy and by mid-1977 a total of

275 had been admitted. However, the Academy is not primarily a flight training facility, but an institution of higher learning much like any other college or university.

4

Personal Traits That Help Make a Pilot

Flying experience, good health and education are absolute necessities for those who hope to become the captains of tomorrow's airliners.

But when airlines consider applicants for their own rosters of pilots, they seek persons with some extra special personal qualifications and characteristics. Among other things these men and women are expected to be:

• Highly motivated—"self-propelled," as one veteran administrative pilot put it. The individual must demonstrate that he or she is truly interested in pilot professionalism and not just interested in qualifying for a job that pays well. Generally speaking, this is evidenced by the person's background—when he or she began flying, hours flown, kinds of planes handled, aviation jobs held, efforts to upgrade abilities, and so on.

• Someone who reacts well under stressful situations. Usually this will be determined in the airline's own retraining process after an applicant has been accepted.

PERSONAL TRAITS THAT HELP MAKE A PILOT

- A person who gets along well with other people, especially in the cockpit. After all, it's rather close quarters in there and the crew sometimes spends hours together on long flights. People who get on each other's nerves don't make the best of flight teams. Today's jets require the ultimate in teamwork.
- One who can assimilate extremely complex information from several different sources. This is regarded as critical because a pilot is getting information simultaneously from his eyes, ears and sense of feel. "He's got to pull all this together and make sense out of it," as another airline official described it.
- Someone who has good reasoning ability. He or she not only has to recognize the information conveyed by the senses but integrate it with experience and training, and make the right decision.
- Someone who is emotionally stable. A pilot who might fall apart in a critical situation isn't exactly the right kind of pilot to have in the captain's seat.
- A person who can plan ahead. A large proportion of flying is concerned with anticipating what will be done in the flight, both soon and later on.
- A person, hopefully, also, with a good deal of mechanical aptitude. A pilot deals with extraordinarily complicated mechanical and electronic devices. He or she must know how to use them.

While each airline establishes its own sets of qualifications for acceptance of pilot applicants, these tend to be quite similar and in many cases identical.

A mighty 747 Luxury Liner on takeoff. (American Airlines)

PERSONAL TRAITS THAT HELP MAKE A PILOT

As an example, here are the minimum initial qualifications set forth by American Airlines:

Age—21. No maximum age is specified by the airline, but the retirement age is 60. Obviously, the nearer one approaches that age the less chance one has. A prime consideration of an airline, at least in normal times, is the investment the carrier has in a pilot's retraining for airliner service and other aspects of his or her career with the line. While this is a great deal less than the Air Force's training cost, it still runs into many thousands of dollars. In considering an applicant, an airline carefully takes into account the number of years the pilot may be able to fly. In other words, the more the better.

Height—5'6" to 6'4". Here is one of the two instances where a woman could be at a disadvantage even though her other qualifications were equal to those of men. Some excellent women pilots are, unfortunately for them, shorter than the 5'6" minimum. Thus they might not readily be able to reach pedal controls.

Strength—the average airline passenger might not ordinarily think of this as being of particular importance, considering the many power-driven controls on modern aircraft. But some planes, particularly the 707, require considerable physical strength on the part of the pilot at times when the craft is under manual control. So pilot applicants must take strength tests too. Hardly ever are these a problem for men, but occasionally they are for women.

Weight—in proportion to height.

Vision—20/20 without glasses, each eye separately. However, minor astigmatic errors may be considered acceptable.

AIRLINE PILOT

Education—college degree or equivalent. The major is not specified, nor are any particular courses required, but extra consideration is given applicants who possess some knowledge of such things as math, trigonometry, mechanics, electronics, aerodynamics, engineering.

Ratings—an FAA commerical-type pilot certificate with an instrument rating. The applicant must also have passed a written basic flight engineer's examination, which is called FEB, and a similar examination for jet engineers, called FEX, or hold a certificate as a jet flight engineer. This is because *all* new pilots for the airline must begin their service as flight engineers. Flight engineer training is not available in the Air Force. It must be obtained through experience elsewhere, or through a special training program which can be taken at one's own expense from some concern other than the airline.

Health—a First Class FAA Medical Certificate is required. No waivers are permitted.

Other—a Federal Communications Commission radiotelephone operator permit.

Citizenship—there are no restrictions. Preference is given to applicants whose natural language is English but any alien who speaks English effectively may be considered. While most recruits are hired from the United States, citizens from other countries sometimes are accepted. These are chiefly from Canada and England.

All that one need do to seek pilot employment with an airline is to write the line at one of its major bases, enclosing a résumé, or appear in person and fill out an application form. In the latter case, questions on the form will cover the applicant's personal, educational and professional qualifications and experience.

After that, all one can do is wait. At the present time the wait could be a long one. There are many more eligible pilots available than openings for them.

5

How Airlines Screen Prospective Pilots

Nowadays the major airlines are blessed by an abundance of riches—in the sense that they have so many highly qualified military and commercial pilots to choose from.

In one recent instance a line decided to fill about 100 openings for future pilots. It had on file thousands of applications. And every applicant seemingly had outstanding qualifications.

As can well be imagined, the subsequent screening process took doing aplenty. Eventually 104 pilots were hired. In choosing that group, the airline interviewed 628 persons.

First, airline personnel made a careful check of all the applications on file. From these were selected the names of the most desirable prospects, judging on the basis of background and experience. After that, the process continued in this fashion:

PHASE 1. Applicants were notified and, if they were still interested, asked to appear at regional bases of the airline in areas where they resided. Interviews were conducted there

HOW AIRLINES SCREEN PROSPECTIVE PILOTS

by regional recruiters for the company.

PHASE 2. Applicants then deemed the most suitable were sent to the company's training facility in a midwestern city for medical and other tests. The medical examination is a stringent one.

PHASE 3. Those who passed the examination were given what are called "flight department interviews"—conducted by veteran pilots—and put through cockpit simulator tests. These are the critical portions of the screening process.

The interviews are conducted at great length and in depth. By the time the interviewers finish with a candidate they will be very well acquainted with his professionalism and personality.

As a further check, however, the prospect is put in a cockpit simulator which most nearly duplicates the plane the pilot is most familiar with. Before being asked to demonstrate flying skills in the simulator, the applicant is given a refresher briefing on operation of the particular plane the simulator represents.

Thereafter the applicant is put through various exercises such as takeoffs and landings, handling the plane under unfavorable weather conditions and coping with different kinds of problems which could arise. Performance is graded in the particular categories.

PHASE 4. A selection board considers all the prospective pilots on the basis of what has been learned, then votes to select those regarded as most worthy. The selection board is made up of experts from the airline's personnel, medical and flight departments, plus advisers to those who actually do the voting.

The American Airlines Flight Academy near the Dallas/Fort Worth Airport. Here even veteran pilots must go through retraining after joining the airline, and also return for periodic checkups. (American Airlines)

Speaking of the stringency of the medical examination, one description of it is that "a hangnail is about the most you can get away with."

A slight heart murmur or a suspected tendency toward diabetes in later life or a tiny hearing defect could be grounds for rejection.

The future airline seniority of those finally selected for service is established in the screening and approval process. No two pilots will ever have the same seniority, even though several may be hired on the same day and only minutes apart.

As each is chosen, he or she will be assigned a seniority number and thus each person hired will outrank the next. This could have considerable importance to some individuals in the years to follow.

For example, if openings for 15 captains suddenly developed, a copilot who was number 16 in seniority would have to bide his time for the next upgrading program. There have been cases where this took a year or even years.

Another important aspect of the screening process is that interviewers will question the prospective pilot closely as to what he does in his nonflying time.

Is the applicant devoting a substantial part of his time to aviation activities, insofar as possible, maintaining flying skills and keeping abreast of technological developments?

Some pilots operate businesses not related to aviation, or pursue other business activities or occupations. Some are interested in investments.

The purpose of ascertaining the extent of these activities is to determine whether the applicant's chief interest lies in them despite flying skills possessed and a profession of great interest in becoming an airline captain.

In other words, an airline doesn't want a pilot who regards flying as something of a money-making hobby or sideline which may be secondary to other pursuits.

Flying must be number one and no doubt about it.

6

Pilot Retraining by the Airlines

No matter how much flight experience a person has had, he or she will have to go back to flight school again once accepted by a major airline.

One won't find any snap courses there, either. In fact, it may prove to be the most demanding training activity yet encountered. Even a veteran pilot will in effect be starting all over again, beginning with the basics. This is because airlines want their pilots to be totally familiar with the planes they'll eventually fly, and to fly them exactly as the company wants them flown.

"Rugged," "tough," "hard work," "whew!" and "what a workout!" are some of the descriptions given by trainees afterward. Very few fail, however, since they have the background to master the studies.

Most airlines have their own training academies whose activities are essentially the same. One of the largest and best equipped is that of American Airlines, located near the Dallas/Fort Worth Airport. It resembles a small college campus, and pilot studies proceed there day and night.

Back in 1966 American began a new approach to pilot training and since then has pioneered many developments in procedures—particularly through a systems approach in ground training facilities and simulators. Formerly much of the instruction took place during actual flight.

American credits its modernized instruction program with enabling it to compile the finest safety record in the history of commercial aviation. Says an American spokesman, "No other human endeavor carries with it responsibilities and complexities comparable to those assumed by the professional flight crewman.

"The basic skills he brings to the job of flying a modern high performance airliner must be tuned to the finest degree. He must function with quickness and precision. The specialized knowledge necessary to meet these requirements must be learned swiftly, completely and indelibly.

"With safety being a total commitment, we have made effective training a total commitment, too."

Describing its procedures in another way, American says that most other kinds of training programs outside aviation basically load students with much more than they can retain, with the hope that they'll remember a reasonable proportion of the important matters.

The airline says it seeks to teach the important things in such a way as to insure retention of close to 100 percent of all of them.

Newcomers as well as the airline's 4,000-plus flight crewmen can be put through as many as 75 different types of

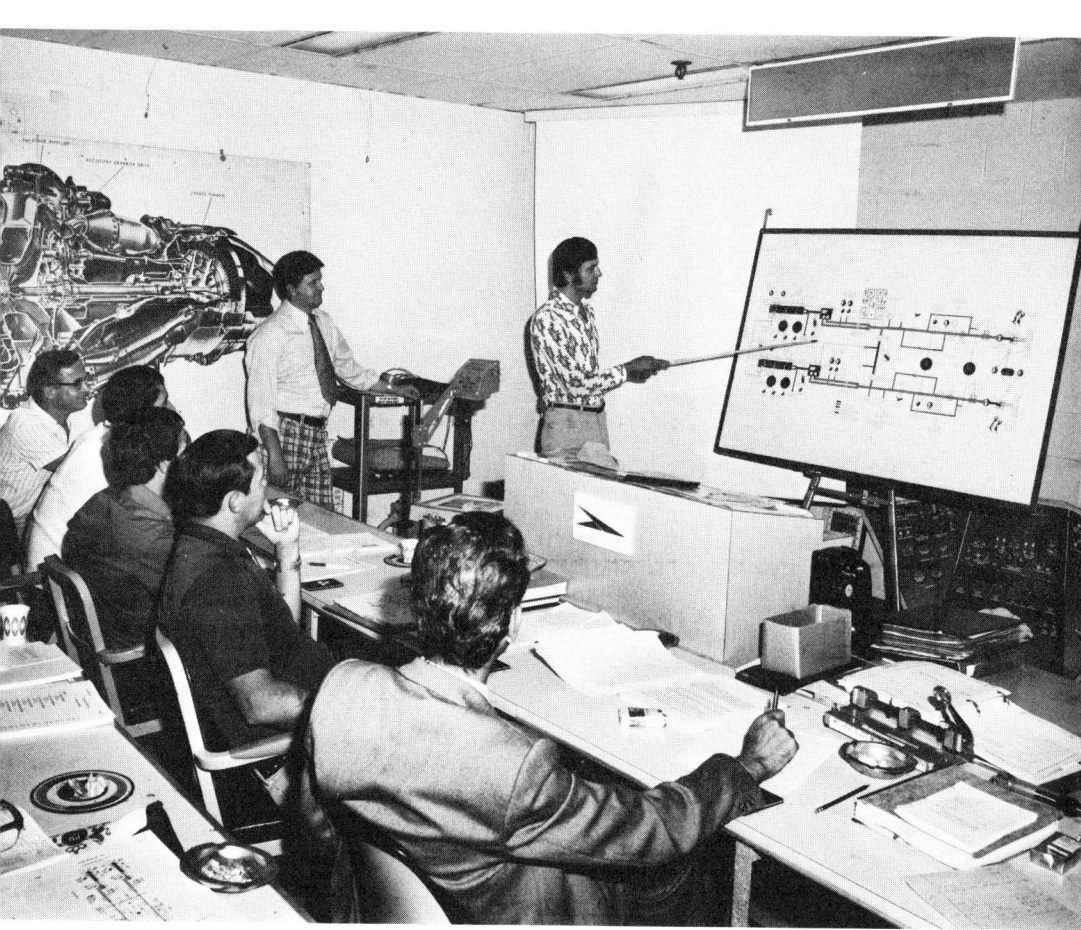

It's back to school again for pilots in an airline retraining course on aircraft systems operation. (Allegheny Airlines)

ground school and flight courses, all approved by the Federal Aviation Administration. Flight crewmen already in service must return periodically for checkouts.

After a newcomer has passed his or her medical examination, ground school work begins. This will cover everything relating to the operation of a jetliner—its construction, systems, instruments and handling, plus related matters such as meteorology, navigation, normal and abnormal operating conditions, emergency procedures and company flight rules.

Each student receives extremely close supervision, sometimes with one instructor per student or at other times per one or two students. However, students are not under pressure to proceed at a fast learning pace. They are permitted to progress at their individual rates.

A key part of initial training is student work in an individual "study unit." This is done in a private enclosure with computerized audio-visual equipment. Through use of slides and motion pictures projected on a screen, the workings of various aircraft system parts can be displayed and questions posed concerning them. The student responds by means of an electronic answer panel. If a correct answer is given, the study display continues with other training questions.

After completion of this phase of training, the student goes to a working mock-up of a particular system for what is called a "hands-on" application of what has been learned. This duplicates the controls of an aircraft relating to that system. It shows the system's operation by using logic circuits to activate color-coded schematic diagrams, mechanical movements, indicator lights and so forth in response to movement of the controls.

In essence, the student is shown cause and effect in graphic fashion, a decided adjunct to problem-solving exercises which follow.

The next step is to the Cockpit Procedures Trainer (CPT). This is an exact reproduction of an actual cockpit, with all controls and instruments for the systems previously studied individually. The student here gets the chance to "put it all together."

The CPT enables the trainees to become better acquainted with locations of controls, switches and components. In addition, they become involved with checklist activities, normal and abnormal procedures, and development of crew coordination skills. The goal is mastery of all systems and their interrelationships, as would be necessary in actual flight.

Finally, the student progresses to simulators which reproduce actual conditions of flight, normal and abnormal. These duplicate cockpits in every respect. A television projection screen, seen through the cockpit windows, can display a view of terrain just as seen by a cockpit crew in takeoffs, landings and in flight. The scene changes just as it would in flight.

There are simulators for the 707 (100 and 300 series), 727 (100 and 200 series), DC-10 and 747. The newcomer will use only the 727. The others are for line pilots getting their periodic checkouts, or in upgrading from one cockpit position to another or to a larger plane.

These simulators are wonders to behold. They reproduce

all aspects of flight so faithfully, including what the crew sees, that it is difficult to believe they're really on the ground all the time.

What makes everything so realistic is that the cockpit crew is treated to all the noises of flight as well as thumps, bumps, wind and weather effects. The only thing not built in is the feel of G-forces. A massive array of hydraulic devices beneath the cockpit creates the motion effects.

The simulator, of course, is a highly computerized mechanism. Virtually anything that any plane ever goes through can be programmed into it, if indeed it hasn't already.

Flight training in the simulator is supervised by veteran captains and flight engineers averaging more than 20 years with the airline and having 15,000 to 20,000 hours of flying experience.

The means of creating the cockpit view is a marvel all unto itself. It is done in each case with a television camera which is aimed at a huge reproduction of terrain with miniature buildings, trees, roads, hills, rivers, highways, lakes and airport runways.

The camera moves up and down, from side to side or far from or near to the surface of the simulated terrain, in response to the way the cockpit controls are handled. Thus the pilot trainee's view from the cockpit will be precisely what he would see in actual flight during takeoffs, normal flight, unusual conditions, turns, descent, airport approaches and landings.

Visibility conditions of all kinds can be, and are, duplicated in the training. Landings and takeoffs, along with other aspects of flight, are carried out under varying aircraft weight and wind conditions, and during daylight, dusk or darkness. All kinds of pseudo emergency situations can be set up for training purposes.

If at any point the trainee is not performing his tasks satisfactorily, the instructor can punch a button and "freeze" everything for a discussion with the student. Through the computer the instructor also can "back up" the procedure and have the trainee run through the exercise again.

Airlines have found this simulator training to hold some extraordinary benefits. For one thing, the trainee can be put through extremely critical emergency conditions without any fear of crashes or damage to aircraft as might occur during training with a real plane. Such things have happened in years long past.

Another virtue is that in a plane there is no control over conditions which may prevail: winds and weather, other air traffic, visibility, gross weight of aircraft and other factors. All that can be done is "take what you get." For this reason many students might never get a chance to encounter some conditions in practice flights. With a simulator any condition can be created.

There are other benefits. Use of actual planes is becoming an increasingly expensive consideration, through fuel and other costs. Moreover, a plane in use for training isn't carrying passengers and making money.

American estimates it is saving enough fuel each year to operate approximately six 707s for a full year.

Still, pilot training isn't actually completed until a person demonstrates a high degree of ability in the real thing. So there will come a time when the trainee takes a cockpit seat

AIRLINE PILOT

in a 727. Alongside as copilot will be a veteran pilot-instructor and an FAA inspector.

Under their sharp eyes the hopeful airline-pilot-to-be will perform takeoffs and landings, and demonstrate plane-handling competence in other designated maneuvers. The checkout ordinarily will take only two hours or so. One trainee is reported to have qualified himself in forty-five minutes.

Successful completion of the training by no means signals that the young pilot will step right in to command an airliner, with big pay and other benefits. There's a long flight yet to be made, so to speak, before he or she attains the lofty pinnacle of captaincy.

The airline newcomer begins the flight career as a flight engineer on a 727. This is a relatively new program of operation by major airlines. There are two prime reasons for it. One is that the airline now has a third duly qualified pilot in the cockpit as a reserve for some unforeseen emergency disabling one of the others. The other is that the flight engineer's job will make the fledgling pilot even more versant with the plane's operation and give him experience which will be valuable after he moves to copilot or pilot status.

As flight engineer the newcomer may have to "fly sideways"—as the flying fraternity puts it—for some time before having a chance to advance to the first officer, or copilot, position. The flight engineer is called the second officer.

The new flight engineer will not find initial pay overwhelming. With American, it's about $1,100 a month for the first 12 months, though there can be additional pay for such things as night flying and international trips over water. Pay will increase materially as seniority is gained.

In time, seniority also will enable the new cockpit hand to move on into the copilot's seat and eventually the captain's. How long this takes depends on many circumstances, such as the airline's need and the openings created by retirement, disability or death in the line's ranks.

Some present pilots had to wait years to make captain. Others, in luckier circumstances, attained the position relatively quickly. As of the time this was written, American Airlines applicants were being told they might have to wait 15 years before they could become captain, but that it could happen sooner.

Whatever position held in the cockpit, each person is subject to periodic retraining at the Dallas/Fort Worth Flight Academy. Captains must return twice a year and first officers and flight engineers once. They also get new physical examinations at the time.

Any cockpit crew member who wishes to qualify for a different plane must go for a retraining program. It also is required when anyone wishes to shift back to another type of plane flown previously but not for a long while.

Needless to say, many beginning airline pilots set their sights on making captain of the 747 eventually. Quite understandably, too. After all, it's the biggest and most impressive thing going.

7

Here Come the Women—Again

There is nothing new about women's flying airplanes, even big ones—except that they now have just as much chance to become jetliner pilots as men, if equally qualified. Their only problem for the moment is that they have a much more difficult time gaining the experience necessary to be accepted by a major airline.

Some of the very first flyers in the world were women. The Wright brothers had hardly gotten their first rickety flying machines off the ground before the women were flying them too.

A woman who died recently saw one of the early aviators demonstrate a clumsy craft in a midwestern cow pasture when she was in her teens. She was much intrigued. So she wrote an eastern company which offered a similar plane disassembled, and ordered one.

By and by the local train came in one day with a boxcar full of crates. The girl uncrated the plane parts, put the machine together and took off. She never took a flying lesson.

"I figured I could do anything a man could do," said she. And so have others ever since. Their record has been as good as men's, too, it would appear.

Many people today tend to forget that women were ferrying bombers and other craft around the country and across the ocean during World War II. Their glory days faded quickly thereafter, because the budding airline business would consider only men for cockpit crews.

A new day has dawned for women now, though, under equal employment opportunity laws. They're making the most of it, with even higher hopes for the future, although the ranks of those in flight are still relatively thin.

The publication *Aviation Daily* reported in mid-1977 that there were only 22 female flight deck officers working for scheduled U.S. airlines out of a total pilot force of approximately 40,000. Foreign carriers, other than in Russia, employed 10 female pilots and 1 flight engineer. Aeroflot, the Soviet airline, was known to have several women pilots but would not divulge the number, evidently regarding it as a state secret.

Typical of America's "new breed" in the cockpit is Mrs. Claudia Jones. She was among the first three women to qualify as a pilot for Continental Airlines. She got her ticket early in 1977, at age 32, and went right to work as second officer, or flight engineer, on a 727. She won't be content until she makes captain of a DC-10, the largest plane Continental operates.

When Mrs. Jones made application to Continental she had more than 5,000 hours of flying time, over 10 years, in dozens of different types of planes. They ranged from her first small single-engine craft through seaplanes, multi-engine piston planes and piston- and jet-driven helicopters.

She said Continental put her through a very rigorous program of training for the 727, but that she was so eager to learn to fly it she didn't mind the hard work.

"Going from smaller planes to larger was challenging. The systems were like nothing I had ever been through before. I did a lot of extra studying on my own," she says.

"I want to know everything there is to know about that airplane, more than just what I have to know. I'd go out there and put on a mechanic's suit and work on it if they'd let me."

Mrs. Jones got into her flying career for an unusual reason—because of her musical ability. She sings and plays nineteen musical instruments. As a music major at the University of Florida she had planned to become a music teacher. But in 1967 she and a friend decided to form a nightclub act. With three backup musicians they began touring the country.

"We had so many problems with transportation somebody decided that one of us would have to learn to fly. Because I was the biggest daredevil they pointed a finger at me."

The others paid for her flying lessons and the group leased a seven-passenger plane, with the back seats removed for carrying their instruments.

In time "flying got to be more fun than entertaining," although she occasionally still does shows between airline schedules. In 1970 she began a new career as a flight

HERE COME THE WOMEN—AGAIN

instructor and charter pilot. This subsequently led to marriage and the presidency of Oasis Aviation, Inc., at Las Vegas, Nevada.

Oasis, co-owned by her husband, Hal Jones, is a fixed-base aviation operation which handles aircraft maintenance, flight instruction, charter flights and aircraft sales. The two met when Jones asked her to teach flying to one of his five children from a previous marriage. Eventually she taught all of them, ranging in age from 13 to 22.

Mrs. Jones said she never went around "knocking on airlines' doors, because they just weren't hiring women." But, she says, "when I heard they were giving women equal opportunity I applied right away." That was in 1976.

"My husband is a ten-thousand-hour pilot, both fixed-wing and helicopter. He had an opportunity about ten years ago to go with the airline and he didn't take it. He has been kicking himself ever since. He told me he wasn't going to let me make the same mistake."

She was the only woman in her training class, which had 17 men.

"They treated me like one of the guys. To date I have not found anyone who's not been really super. I heard that there would be some who would give me a hard time but nobody has. They've been very helpful; in fact, just great."

She has received startled looks aplenty from others, however.

"After I walk off the airplane, or I'm walking around on the ground making the plane inspection before flight, the guys who are fueling the aircraft really give me some odd stares.

"I had one really surprised passenger. He looked in the

cockpit and exclaimed, 'A *girl?*' All I said was 'Here I am.' He laughed, said, 'I sure don't believe it,' and walked away."

There are a couple of small ways in which male and female airline officers' situations will always differ somewhat.

One is the matter of uniform. While Mrs. Jones' uniform is otherwise identical to those of the fellows, her double-breasted coat is fitted and has four buttons instead of six. She also wears a softer shirt with no pockets. Her hair is pulled back at the neck and underneath the regulation cap.

The 5'7" brown-eyed blonde began her career with Continental as a reserve pilot based in Los Angeles. Being on reserve means being on call for a certain number of days each month to fill in for other flight engineers on vacation, ill or otherwise unable to make their runs.

On days off her husband sometimes flies one of their company's planes to join her in Los Angeles, or she flies to join him in Las Vegas. They have a home twenty miles northwest of Las Vegas on an 8,500-foot level in the Toyabee National Forest. In Los Angeles she shares an apartment with one of the other two Continental women crew members.

Flying reserve delighted Mrs. Jones because the trips varied greatly, giving her a chance to see many different cities. Continental covers a large portion of the western half of the country, with runs also to Miami and Hawaii.

Generally speaking, however, she wasn't getting much time for sightseeing—or shopping—in other cities because the layover time usually was only enough to sleep and rest before making the return trip.

Her longest run was to Miami from Los Angeles. That required about 6 hours of actual flying and a total duty time of 8 with stops along the way.

Many of her flights were at night. In some ways she likes night flying best: "It's no more difficult to fly at night. Actually it's easier to spot other airplanes, because of their lights, and airports are easier to find. It's smoother flying, too, because the air has calmed down."

Mrs. Jones finds little difference in flying small planes or large ones. On the large craft the controls are boosted hydraulically, as with power steering in an automobile, so that the plane responds to controls like the smaller ones do.

To some it might seem that there would be great differences because of the higher landing speeds of the jetliners, and because the cockpit is so much higher from the ground. The way of compensating for these effects, says Mrs. Jones, is easy. The larger and faster the aircraft, the farther down the runway you look. That puts everything in the same perspective as for a smaller plane.

Is there any real difference between men and women when it comes to flying?

"People have preconceived notions, and it will take a little time to change all that.

"I've taught men to fly and I've taught women to fly, and I honestly cannot see any difference in ability."

The new era for women in American aviation dawned in January 1973. It was then that Emily H. Warner became the first woman pilot in the nation's airline industry. She's now a captain. She made the top rank in four years.

Captain Warner was hired by Frontier Airlines as second

Emily Warner, first woman pilot hired by a scheduled U.S. airline and first to become a captain. (Frontier Airlines)

officer. At the time she had been flying 15 years and had 7,000 flying hours to her credit.

Like that of Claudia Jones, Emily Warner's path to an airline pilot's career is a perfect example of what veteran skippers and airline operations people recommend for those who take the civilian route. As a teenager she wanted to become a flier—and so she did.

Ms. Warner, a native of Colorado, took her first airplane trip in the mid-1950s on a Frontier flight from Durango to Denver. This spurred her interest in aviation and she thought of becoming a stewardess. However, a Frontier pilot suggested that she think about taking flying lessons instead. In 1958 she began.

She earned a private pilot's license in a year, then took more lessons to acquire a commercial license and an instructor's rating. In 1960 she joined the Clinton Aviation Company near Denver. There she taught students seeking private and commercial licenses until 1963, when she completed requirements for her own instrument-flight rating, then began giving instrument lessons.

By 1966 she had become Clinton's assistant flight school manager and a flight training specialist. Two years later she received her ratings from the FAA as a flight examiner and airline transport pilot. In 1969 she was made Clinton's flight school manager and chief pilot.

After her pioneering feat of winning pilot's wings from Frontier in 1973 she received the Amelia Earhart Award as the year's outstanding woman in U. S. aviation. The next year she became the first woman to be elected to membership in the Air Line Pilots Association.

AIRLINE PILOT

Today Captain Warner has more than 9,000 hours in her logbook and is one of Frontier's 550 pilots. The airline links more than 100 cities in 17 western states and Manitoba, Canada.

After serving a period as flight engineer on Frontier's 737 jetliners, Captain Warner became a first officer on Convair 580 propjets and deHavilland Twin Otter DHC-6 planes, also propjets. On June 1, 1976, she was advanced to captain on the Twin Otter.

"All I've ever wanted to do since I was seventeen was fly," says Captain Warner.

"When I started working for Frontier it felt good and it felt strange at the same time. For the first year the other pilots watched me to see what I could do. Now, after four years, the men I work with treat me like another pilot.

"Teamwork in the cockpit is extremely important. You work as a team and after a while you just forget that man-woman business.

"There is no position in commercial aviation unsuitable for women. While we probably never will be the majority among flight crews, the time will come when women will be accepted without question on equal basis with men in all positions, judged solely on ability."

The Silver-Winged Women

And so, into the wild blue yonder also went the first women ever to be trained as military pilots by the United States Air Force.

There were 10 of them, along with 39 men, in a class which began flight training at Williams Air Force Base on September 29, 1976. Some were plain scared of the formidable task they knew they faced; some doubted their ability to survive it; all were nervous.

In the ensuing months they found their apprehension well justified. It was no easy, gentle process such as some had encountered in training for private pilots' licenses. It was work—hard, tough and at times agonizing. Some found it, physically and emotionally, the greatest ordeal they'd ever been through.

There were tears, deep depression and occasionally the temptation to give up. Tension and utter weariness abounded. And could the human mind absorb one bit more of the massive technical knowledge yet to be mastered in hours upon hours of classwork?

But with true grit, they stuck to it. And when graduation day finally arrived on September 2, 1977, all 10 proudly marched up to receive their silver wings as Air Force pilots.

Few women were ever so delighted by their deeds. They had matched their male counterparts in one of the most rugged training programs on earth and had come through with banners aflutter.

In some ways they did even better than the men. One of the women, Connie J. Engel, soon a captain, was the top student in the class. And three of the men who began the class had fallen by the wayside. One was washed out, one dropped for medical reasons, and a third set back a class.

However, 10 women in a second class did not fare so well. Three were washed out and another decided she'd rather return to her previous job as an Air Force physical therapist.

After graduation, the first group of women immediately went into other Air Force flight activities or advanced training. Captain Engel decided on a career as a flight instructor. As such she'd be teaching men and perhaps other women.

Others set about learning to fly such aircraft as the four-engine C-141 Starlifter, a jet used to transport military cargo around the world; the KC-135, a tanker version of the Boeing 707 used to refuel B-52 bombers; and the C-9, the Air Force version of the DC-9, employed as a medical evacuation plane and for other purposes.

The first 20 women pilot trainees ranged in age from 22 to 28. Seventeen already were Air Force officers, 1 was in the Air National Guard and 1 in the Air Force Reserve. Three of the original 10 were wives of Air Force officers and the others were single.

A C-141 shown in flight against a spectacular backdrop. (U.S. Air Force)

AIRLINE PILOT

* * *

The first female trainees served to some degree as guinea pigs for the Air Force to ascertain how things would go during integrated training. However, Captain Gene Harbula, who was in charge of monitoring the program, said that no great trouble was encountered.

The only problem of any consequence, he said, was in finding flying equipment to fit them. This was solved by custom-tailoring their flight suits.

At different times during the training 8 or 10 were placed on "marginal" status, meaning that they were having difficulty. But this was not any higher rate than for the men in the class, Captain Harbula said.

"It was tough on them, like it is on the men, but they all wanted badly to succeed.

"When we went into it we expected to see more tears, and I must admit in all frankness we did see a few more tears than we do with the guys.

"But it's not unusual for the men to cry when things go wrong, and we did the same thing we do with the men: if you see somebody starting to cry after a bad ride, you just say, 'Do you want five minutes by yourself, or would you like to go have a Coke?'

The women themselves were quick to attest to the rigorous nature of the program.

"Physically and emotionally," says Captain Kathy LaSauce, a 27-year-old blonde from Medford, New York, "pilot training is the toughest thing to go through that you can image—and I mean that without exaggeration."

She ought to know. Earlier in life she had tackled another

THE SILVER-WINGED WOMEN

one in which few succeed. She had majored in drama at Ithaca College and had a glorious dream of making Broadway. Unhappily for her, the dream proved only that.

So in 1972 Kathy entered the Air Force officer training program. After receiving her commission she was assigned to Guam and supervised a maintenance unit for C-141 transports.

"It looked pretty romantic to see those guys climbing in those jets and taking off to places around the world," she recalls. "When I heard they were going to accept women I applied to be a pilot. For a career, it also helps to have wings on your chest."

How did she find the training?

"We all went into deep depressions at times, but we tried to keep our spirits up. I decided if you let a bad ride affect you, then your confidence is gone.

"I decided what made some pilots better than others was self-confidence. Once I convinced myself I was good, I started doing okay."

Captain Engle, 28 and also a vivacious blonde who lists her home as Lompoc, California, was literally surrounded by family pilots but had never considered becoming one herself.

Her father is a retired Air Force lieutenant colonel and her husband is an Air Force test pilot assigned to Edwards Air Force Base in California. A sister and brother-in-law also fly.

Instead, Captain Engel had been an obstetrics-gynecology nurse at Randolph Air Force Base near San

A KC-135 tanker refuels an EC-145 Airborne Command Post high above the clouds. (U.S. Air Force)

Antonio, Texas. She had earned a bachelor's degree in nursing science from the University of Texas and subsequently entered the Air Force through direct appointment in 1971.

"I never really thought about flying until about six months before I started the pilot training program. My husband was working on the project for women's pilot training. He was very excited about it and we talked about it for a long time.

"I had just never considered that I'd be able to fly any plane, even though the others in my family were pilots. To me, that was up there and I was down here and I didn't think I could ever do something that complicated.

"But the more my husband and I talked about it the more interested I became. He was an instructor pilot when we first met, and I thought, 'Well, if I've got my own instructor pilot at home and I go through the program, maybe I can make it.'

"He said, 'Well, you don't even know if you want to fly. Why don't you go and try—get your private pilot's license and see if you like it.' Six weeks later I had my private license. I really liked to fly. It was fun. I didn't find it too terribly complicated so I said, 'Well, I think I will do it.' So I applied to the Air Force."

Was it fun too?

"It was the most difficult thing I've ever done. It was a year of extremely long hours, extreme stress, a lot of things to do and a lot of technical things to learn. If I took all my nursing and packed it into one year instead of four I might be able to compare it.

"Many times I went through the 'Gee, what am I doing

here?' syndrome. But I don't think I ever felt that I would fail at it. It was very difficult, but the rough spots were gotten through quickly enough that I never had a sense of fear that I would fail.

"I think the hardest thing is trying to organize your time, trying to find the right time for everything and not to waste time. Get your flying in, get your studying in, get your eating in, get your rest in. Find some time to relax so that you can do it all again the next day.

"I found that Friday evenings were 'my' time of the week and just about the only time that I could do absolutely nothing—go home and have dinner and watch TV and go to sleep early."

And what did she find to be the most troublesome thing of all in handling aircraft?

"Landing."

Captain Susan D. Rogers, 27, was both a private pilot and Air Force nurse. The captain, from Wilmington, Delaware, had previously logged some 250 hours in civilian aircraft and held multiengine and instrument ratings.

She started learning to fly at 22 out of curiosity. "It was just something I wanted to try. I thought it would be something fun to do."

However, she never seriously considered making a career of it. Instead, after receiving a diploma in nursing she entered the Air Force through direct appointment in 1972. She was stationed as a general medical ward nurse at an Air Force hospital in England when the opportunity for military flight training arose.

Captain Rogers jumped at the chance for the same reason most airline pilots seek to upgrade themselves: "It was an opportunity to fly larger aircraft."

The quiet-spoken brunette, who is single, found that the opportunity was not without its rocky aspects, too.

Interviewed in New York with Captain Engel during an Air Force promotional visit shortly after graduation, Captain Rogers said also, "It was the hardest thing I've ever done. There were times when I thought 'maybe I won't.' "

One thing that gave her particular trouble was flying what is called the "cloverleaf." This involves a complicated series of maneuvers in going up, turning, going down . . . up again, turn, down, and so on.

At times Captain Rogers also suffered from cases of what often bedevils even veteran airline pilots. It's what they call "checkitis." Things have a way of seeming to go sour whenever there's an inspector along to check out a pilot's performance.

Like others in the class, both captains found that time was a premium commodity.

Captain Rogers: "You've got about a twelve- or fourteen-hour day on the flight line and in academics. Then, they like you to get eight hours sleep at night. You try to find time to eat and study, and you still have to do some washing and tend to other things, and throughout all this maintain some semblance of mental health."

Captain Engel: "I got used to sleeping four or five hours. Most of the time I'd try to catch up on weekends."

Captain Rogers: "I need more than that. I went on about six or seven. I took Saturdays for myself and then studied all day Sunday, trying to catch up on what went on the last week and trying to prepare for the next week."

Others with Captains LaSauce, Engel and Rogers in the history-making women's group were Captain Mary E. Donahue, of Boston, Massachusetts, and First Lieutenants Victoria K. Crawford, also of Lompoc, California; Mary M. Livingston, Manistique, Michigan; Christine E. Schott, Indiana, Pennsylvania; Sandra May Scott, Forest Grove, Oregon; Carol Ann Scherer, Springfield, Oregon; and Second Lieutenant Kathleen A. Rambo, Arlington, Virginia.

All draw regular pay for their ranks plus an extra payment for flying. This begins at about $100 a month and increases with experience to a maximum of $245.

While Captain Engel elected to become a career flight instructor, Captain Rogers chose to train as pilot for the C-9 and Captain LaSauce as pilot for the C-141 Starlifter.

In time the women who train on the larger Air Force planes probably could qualify for acceptance by commerical airlines. However, Captains Engel and Rogers perhaps reflected the thoughts of others in saying they hadn't given the possibility any consideration. In any case, they had four additional years remaining on their Air Force commitment and for the moment were much too entranced with what beckoned in the immediate future.

Asked their views on the possibility of women's eventually flying on combat missions, Captains Engel and Rogers declined to comment, saying that this was a matter for civilian determination.

Several women's organizations have called for repeal of

laws relegating women to noncombat roles in the armed forces. Congressional hearings have been held on the subject but no recommendations have been forthcoming.

An exciting future possibility for women pilots lies in the space shuttle program. The National Aeronautics and Space Administration invited women to apply when it began a recruitment drive for astronauts for the program in 1976.

More than 1,500 did so. However, none was accepted for astronaut-pilot training. NASA explained that, among other qualifications, it preferred women experienced with high-performance jet aircraft and flight testing.

None of the women had such a background—but that isn't to say they won't in the future.

Captains Engel and Rogers have some very positive thoughts about qualifications for becoming a good pilot.

Captain Engel: "I think that in myself I find the qualities that enhance my flying are a certain aggressiveness in many kinds of flying, being very mentally alert, making sure you have things very well organized, trying to keep ahead of the plane. Making sure the airplane doesn't fly you, but you fly the airplane.

"I think I have seen myself over this past year being more outgoing or aggressive."

Captain Rogers: "That and also just some basic common sense. Not everything is going to be in the book. You've got to know your airplane and know the environment you're flying in well enough to make the best judgment you can when situations arise.

"No two flights are going to be the same. There's going to

AIRLINE PILOT

be *something* different about them. You can't stereotype it, you can't pigeonhole it. It's just having the common sense to make decisions and stick with them."

As for advice to those who think they'd like to become pilots, be they women or men, Captain Engel sums it up in short order: "If you want to bad enough, you can do it."

The Pilot's Pilot

Two things, essentially, enabled the stumbling young airlines of the 1930s to get off to a literal flying start toward becoming the giants of today—the DC-3 airplane and pilots like Russell Sapp.

The DC-3 was to become known as the "workhorse" of early commercial aviation. And, truly, that it was. In a way it was much like the Model-T Ford which served a growing nation so well.

The DC-3 carried only 21 passengers and needed a crew of 3 to operate it: pilot, copilot and stewardess. But it was a sturdy plane, economical to operate and dependable. It changed the ink on airline ledgers from red to black. Some of those DC-3s are still in use, both in this country and elsewhere in the world.

Russell Sapp's flying career spanned 34 years and carried him from the days of the DC-2, the less-practical predecessor of the DC-3, well into the big-jet era.

AIRLINE PILOT

He was a boy of 7 in Boise, Idaho, when he first thought he wanted to be a flier. He got that notion when he saw an airplane for the first time. Right after the end of World War I some men came to Boise and put on an air show. Young Russell was agape at the sight. "I thought it was the greatest thing in the world."

However, it was to be many years more before he could begin to fulfill the ambition inspired by the air show, and even then more or less by accident. He was into his twenties without having done more than take a couple of rides in some old barnstorming planes.

"I was a poor boy, didn't have any money and wasn't near to any airports in those days. So I had almost given up ever getting to fly. That was right at the end of the Depression and I had been doing a little of everything. I worked on a ranch out in eastern Oregon for one year, then I drove taxis for a couple of years.

"A buddy of mine came around one day and said, 'Hey, why don't you try to get in the Air Corps?' So I wrote to the Army to get all the information. Then they gave me a chance to take the physical and I had to go to Seattle to take it.

"I got out there and it was Friday the thirteenth. Five of us took the physical and I was the only one that passed. I was twenty-six at the time. I had been out of college four years.

"I just got in by the skin of my teeth. My next birthday was two months later and then I would have been too old. They had some rough officers in those days and they were making bets how long it would be before I washed out."

Far from washing out, Sapp sailed through his Army flight training and on into an aviation career that took him to the

Captain Russell Sapp, the onetime ranchhand who flew everything from early-day airliners to modern jets.

very top rank in seniority with American Airlines. Upon retirement at 60 he was somewhere among the 50 with longest service in the pilot force of some 4,000. As near as he can guess, he flew 5 or 6 million miles as a pilot.

His first Army Air Corps training was in single-engine open cockpit planes that had only four instruments, and they were on the outside of the cockpit. They were an altimeter, oil temperature gauge, tachometer and a fuel gauge in the form of a glass tube.

Some of the aircraft did very well for their time while others, to use a phrase coined many years ago, almost didn't fly.

Sapp was to fly in three wars. After about two years with the Army he joined American because "the airlines were screaming for pilots in those days." Then World War II came on and he was called back to service. He ferried bombers across the Atlantic, did transport service in Africa and later trained pilots in Florida.

Sapp did a lot of flying across the Pacific during the Korean and Vietnam conflicts, with the DC-4 in the former and the 707 in the latter. He was then back with American, which was flying personnel and supplies under contract with the military services.

He says his planes were shot at many times, particularly while flying into and out of Vietnam, but were never hit. However, he had only two such experiences during World War II. Once was when a German submarine fired at him. The other time was when some British forces fired by mistake.

On several trips to Vietnam, Sapp carried cargoes of

THE PILOT'S PILOT

explosive materials. He avers that he probably made his smoothest landings ever on these flights.

During his airline years Sapp progressed through most of the new, bigger and better aircraft as they were developed. He has high praise for the people who have designed and built them.

"The safety of airplanes is not only in the pilot training but also due to the millions of hours of engineering that have gone into the present-day transport airplane, and other airplanes too.

"If it weren't for the skill in building these machines there wouldn't be a one of us pilots, that have flown for thirty-three or thirty-four years as I have, who'd be alive.

"Likewise my hat's off to the pioneer flight personnel who went through all the years of learning, all the accidents and so on, that have given us accumulated experience in flight. Today our safety is a result of it."

What Sapp doesn't say is that he passed along to others years of accumulated experience too. Scores of them are the airline pilots of today.

To this veteran there are some prime things that a flight instructor tries to teach a learner. They are: *Never be in a rush, never take things for granted, never skip a checklist, never rely on your memory—rely on your checklist. The memory can skip.*

"We had a pilot one time who came in and landed on his belly at LaGuardia Airport in New York. What had happened was that when he came in he had to pull up and go around and make another approach. When he pulled up he retracted his landing gear. When he came in for his landing the second time he just forgot to lower his gear again, because he had already been through the checklist once.

"Fortunately, the plane landed on its belly and skidded along, causing slight damage but no injuries."

On further thought, Sapp added one more "never" to his list: *Never take shortcuts.*

There is another important piece of wisdom that Sapp would like to impart to new pilots, especially those flying smaller planes: "One of our old pilots told me one time when I was a young squirt: 'You know, one of the best things to learn about flying is to know when to quit flying.'

"I would suspect that ninety percent of accidents outside of airline flying—flying for pleasure or business—are because of people doing it when they shouldn't, due to weather or other circumstances. They shouldn't be pushing their luck.

"It's a cardinal rule that a person should always observe. That's one of the sagest pieces of advice I ever gleaned from a professional pilot."

Aside from flying airline schedules, Sapp has spent much of his professional time as an instructor, check pilot and administrative operations supervisor.

In these capacities he has seen a great many people come and go, has worked with them, trained them and sometimes had to wash them out—even old friends with long experience. He says that supervisory pilots sometimes ask themselves what kind of an individual it takes to reach the proficiency needed in airline flying. These are some of their thoughts on the matter:

"The first quality that a person really needs above everything else is good, honest self-criticism. A person that can take criticism is one that can be a pilot. One who can't stand to be wrong is one that should never get into flying airplanes.

"It's through our slight little errors that we learn a lot of things. If a man cannot admit his errors he has no place in the air, because that air is an unforgiving factor. Mistakes up there can be fatal.

"I believe the right kind of temperament is another thing which a person needs. A good, stable, even temperament makes for a person's reaching a good degree of professionalism.

"Along with ability to take criticism goes the man who is always willing to learn and is never a smart aleck or know-it-all. When you run into a fellow and start to tell him something, and he tries to go ahead of you and start telling *you*, you'd better go easy with this guy. Don't turn *him* loose with your passengers.

"Unless he has a complete change of personality he's going to have a difficult time some day and make the wrong decision, assuming he's correct when he isn't. He's the kind who will have taken an attitude about things that 'I know this. I don't have to work, study it. I just do this and that's all.' His big problem is that *he doesn't know that he doesn't know*.

"I think possibly a lot of fatal accidents in private flying occur from just this one factor."

A different aspect of airline flying relates to the ability of the people in the cockpit to get along well with each other, Captain Sapp says.

"Personality conflict is a thing that should be completely out the window when it comes to flight. I heard of one accident where several passengers were killed due to conflict of personality.

"The pilot was an old-timer who had learned to fly by the so-called seat of the pants. He had let his old 'expertise' drift on into the modern cockpit. He was a do-it-all-himself type of individual who did not rely on the rest of the crew. As a result there was a crash on a landing. The pilot never got over it."

Captain Sapp says there is another thing which should be emphasized as of special importance for all pilots to learn. That is to rely unfailingly on aircraft instruments and disregard any personal feelings or instincts when they are at variance with the instruments.

"If you don't, you could think you're turning to the right sometimes when you're actually turning to the left. Or that you're descending when you may be climbing, and a host of other things.

"It's difficult to learn this except through hours of training and experience. But you must believe the instruments instead of your seat-of-the-pants feeling. If you don't, you'll never make it to the top in professional flying."

Many pilot trainees do not react well to having someone checking on them as they demonstrate their aircraft handling ability. At best such individuals are resentful and at worst their performance suffers. In his roles as instructor and pilot supervisor, Captain Sapp found that a bit of

THE PILOT'S PILOT

philosophy he first voiced to a young flier years ago seemed to help overcome "checkitis" problems very readily.

The young man was in training on the DC-4. He appeared to be a capable pilot but seemed to have difficulty in learning certain things.

"One day as part of his training I cut an engine on him," the captain related. "He just went all to pieces and gave up.

"I let another trainee take over the captain's seat while I took the fellow having trouble back in the plane to talk to him. I knew he was a much better pilot than the way he was doing, and thought it was time to see if I couldn't straighten him out.

"His problem, it turned out, was that when I cut the engine on him he just couldn't take checking and instruction. He'd just give up. He said he'd had enough checking and that was all there was to it. He was through.

"I sat back there and talked to him a while about this checking business. I said, 'This is just a routine thing like you're going through in everyday life. When you go down to the bank to make a deposit, you fill out the slip and the bank checks it over. This is a check on what you're doing. Actually, when you're walking down the street you're checking on yourself against gravity all the time, although you don't realize it. When you talk to somebody you're constantly checking on the words that you are using to express yourself. You're checking to see whether you're using the right words. All your life is a constant check, one way or another, by you or by others. The reason of it is very simple: because we're not perfect, are we?'

" 'No,' he says, 'we're not.'

" 'We're always having to check on ourselves . . . constantly . . . to see that we're doing a thing correctly, aren't we?'

" 'Yeah, that's right.'

"I proceeded on this course of talking with the young fellow for, I guess, ten or fifteen minutes. Pretty soon he was all settled down and went back up to the captain's seat. He went through his maneuvers and that was the last of the difficulties that he had with this 'checkitis' business."

That kind of philosophy ought to stand anyone in good stead, in flying or any other occupation.

Captain Sapp, who doesn't look his age, is a man of medium build, with a slow but deep and melodious drawl in speaking. He has a twinkle in his eyes and loves to laugh. Passengers must have had fun riding with him, even back in the days when weather made things much more rugged on many flights.

He was forever delighting the customers with kidding little announcements over the intercom.

One time he was checking out another pilot on a run to El Paso. The landing was somewhat bumpy—not seriously so, but the plane went thump, thump, thump. Sapp got on the loudspeaker. "Good afternoon, everyone," he said, "we've just landed at El Paso, El Paso, El Paso. We'll be at the ramp in a moment."

Sapp said the pilot didn't think his remarks any too funny but that the passengers were smiling and laughing as the crew opened the cockpit door.

On another occasion, after his plane had gone through a

severe buffeting in a thunderstorm, Sapp told the passengers, "Sometimes there I thought I was going to have to go to work."

Sapp, who never had a really serious emergency in all his years of flying, says he enjoyed every minute of it.

"I never got tired of looking at the sky and earth. Things are always changing: never the same twice and beautiful all the time.

"No two clouds are alike; the weather is never the same; it's a different day and you've got different experiences to go through. When you're up there going through cloud layers there's always a mystique that's different from every other flight.

"Unless a person is a complete bore to himself, it's one of the most interesting jobs a person could ever have, one of the most exciting. As one of our old pilots used to say when we were sitting around exchanging lies, 'Well, it beats working for a living.'

"Some of those times, though, when you had to dig in and make an instrument landing under adverse conditions, you really made up for the times when it was just fun up there flying."

There is only one thing he has ever been sorry about. He didn't fly the 747. He could have done so, when the planes were put in service about a year and a half before his retirement, but he passed up the chance. Even so, he almost changed his mind at the last minute. Very often since he has regretted that he didn't.

Still, the rewards from such a career continue even in retirement.

There are times when, riding planes as a passenger

AIRLINE PILOT

instead of as the captain in the cockpit, he'll get to thinking he could do a better job than the fellow flying.

"But nevertheless you sit back there, relax and say, 'The guy knows what he's doing, and he's doing it as well as he could. He must be doing it well because I taught him how.'"

10

The New Airliner Captain of Today

D. A. "Tony" Felder is a new jetliner captain who says he likes flying so well he'd even do it for less pay.

It took him 11 years to make it from flight engineer to commander of a 727 but he doesn't begrudge one minute of it. He was 40 years old when he was tapped to take over the controls in January, 1976. His only regret is that because of his age he may never rise high enough in seniority to captain a 747.

Captain Felder's rise through the ranks was, by virtue of circumstances, a little slower than some but much faster than others. He credits military flight training not only for giving him a running start toward an airline career but also for providing discipline at a time when he needed it as a young man.

"I was in college as an engineering student, but not doing well and not happy about it," recounts Felder. "A friend of mine came along all dressed up in a Navy suit. I said, 'What kind of suit is that?' He said, 'I'm an air cadet and if you join the Navy you can be one too.' So I joined.

Captain D. A. "Tony" Felder at the helm of a 727. (American Airlines)

"The discipline that the Navy gave me was exactly what I needed at the time. I was smart enough, I guess, but I just didn't have the discipline for college. I did quite well with the Navy—became a commander in a cadet battalion and was one of the better students. I went through the entire training and never got a 'down.'"

Felder had never flown a plane before joining the Navy. In fact, the only time he'd ever been in one was when a friend took him for a ride in a small craft when he was 16.

Once in the Navy air training program he took on what he considered to be the toughest part of it, learning to be a jet fighter pilot. "I was very proud of myself by the time I got out." The largest plane he flew during service was a two-engine Grumman Albatross.

One Navy experience tested his mettle for continuing as a flier.

"I had a crash, and for a while I was wondering whether I could get back on the horse, but I did. It was in an antisubmarine plane flying off an aircraft carrier. There was a midair collision, which wasn't my fault."

While flying in formation the two planes collided engine to engine. Felder's craft lost its left engine and the other its right. The other plane managed to crash-land at an airport on shore. Felder's landed in a tree in a farmer's field. He was in a hospital for about a month with a broken arm. After this sort of thing, says Felder, some people cannot muster the courage to fly again.

Oddly, it was a movie that prompted Felder to set his sights on becoming an airline pilot.

After leaving the Navy he was knocking around in rather footloose fashion, trying to figure out what he really wanted to do.

Sitting home watching television one night he saw the film *The Spirit of St. Louis*, with Jimmy Stewart portraying Charles A. Lindbergh in his epic solo flight across the Atlantic.

"I thought, 'Hell, I can do that.' All my friends were going with airlines and doing that sort of thing, so that's what I did. In those days—the mid-1960s—the airlines were hiring lots of people. I went for interviews and they seemed like the most pleasant people I'd ever met."

Felder had picked American Airlines, which promptly accepted him as a trainee and put him through three months of schooling on the DC-6. He was getting close to 30 at the time.

For a short time he flew as a flight engineer on the DC-6 and the Electra, a turbojet, then progressed to copilot on a two-engine British-made jet and the 727.

Felder is impressed by the great changes in training facilities and procedures at the Dallas/Fort Worth Flight Academy between the time he began and today.

"Now they have quite a palace compared to the old dinky thing we went through. It's far better with all the aids they have now instead of somebody just drawing on a chalkboard."

Felder remembers with fondness, however, the senior pilot who gave him his first checkout flight on the DC-6. It was none other than Captain Russell Sapp.

"Russ and his contemporaries are my heroes," says Felder. "They helped us new guys not to make the same mistakes they did. All modern-day pilots owe their lives to someone back there who taught painful lessons. Some people didn't make it through the experience.

"Russ and others developed those simulators and other training devices. They gave us many of the procedures we follow. I want Russ to know we haven't forgotten."

Despite an enthusiasm for flying and initial success at it, Felder says, some candidates for airline piloting will find that they're not really suited to it.

"There were people I went through training with who just couldn't stand it. They were either unsure of themselves or the situation, or just didn't have the temperament to maintain whatever steadiness that was required to carry on. Some may have had an experience which frightened them so much they couldn't continue. It's no reflection on character, just that way."

It was men like Russell Sapp who had to ascertain whether yesteryear's applicants had the ability and temperament to succeed—and to make today's pilots out of them if they did.

The tall, ruggedly built Tony Felder, an affable man who conveys an appearance of great inner calmness and steadfastness, depicts himself as much like other boys during his youth. He took part in athletics and "had fun with automobiles and motorcycles." He now likes to fish and sail when he's not flying. Other hobbies are woodworking and music.

"My biggest hobby is sailing, and I believe that is because it is so close to flying. I play the guitar quite badly. As a lad in junior high school I played clarinet. I bought a recorder several years ago, and since the fingering is similar to clarinet, I picked it up rapidly."

For a while the captain had an outside business as agent for a foreign yacht company but gave it up. He didn't immediately take on any other enterprise, though he says there is a need for doing so.

"It is important for us to get some sort of business going for two reasons: (1) Tax shelters and write-offs. Wage earners really get soaked by the Internal Revenue Service and especially in the $50,000 area. [That is Felder's pay. It will increase with seniority.] (2) In case we are medically unable to continue careers. We have some disability insurance but it cannot replace lost earnings if we are retired medically.

"In the same light, we are required by federal regulations to retire at 60. Airplane flying is very specialized business, and once one has been that specialized for twenty years or so it is hard to start over."

Felder lives at North Kingstown, Rhode Island, and in a sense commutes to work by car. His base is at Boston. From there he flies a variety of routes around the country with the 727.

It is about an hour's drive from his home to the Boston airport. When he has an early morning flight out, he often drives to Boston and spends the preceding night there. That way he doesn't take any chance on being delayed in reaching the airport by traffic, car trouble or whatever. When his flight is ready to go he wants to be right where he's supposed to be—in the captain's seat.

Felder, like other airliner captains, must be at the airport

THE NEW AIRLINER CAPTAIN OF TODAY

one hour ahead of flight time to prepare for the trip. So he puts up at a motel next to the airport the night before and leaves his car in the airport parking lot en route to the airline terminal. The next day on return, or in some cases the second day, he can hop in the car quickly and head for home.

Under the airline contract, the maximum scheduled flying time for pilots like Captain Felder is 75 hours a month. However, this can be exceeded in certain cases where necessary.

Before the end of each month Felder will know, through a pilot bidding process, what his flight schedule for the next month will be. That way he can make plans in advance for whatever he wishes to do with his time off.

Here is an example of Captain Felder's flight schedule over a period of several days, with cities and their airline designations shown first:

LGA	LaGuardia, N.Y.	IAH	Houston
DFW	Dallas/Fort Worth	CVG	Cincinnati
BNA	Nashville	BOS	Boston
ORD	Chicago	SAT	San Antonio
YYZ	Toronto	EWR	Newark, N.J.
STL	St. Louis	ELP	El Paso
DCA	Washington, D.C.	DTW	Detroit

Flight No.	From	To	Depart	Arrive	Time	Date
295	BOS	LGA	0700	0817	:52	6/26/77
295	LGA	DFW	0845	1105	3:20	

AIRLINE PILOT

Flight No.	From	To	Depart	Arrive	Time	Date
254	DFW	BNA	0610	0744	1:34	
254	BNA	DCA	0810	1036	1:26	6/27/77
254	DCA	BOS	1105	1223	1:18	
295	BOS	LGA	0705	0755	:50	6/30/77
295	LGA	DFW	0825	1038	3:13	
254	DFW	BNA	0627	0803	1:36	
254	BNA	DCA	0823	1049	1:26	7/1/77
254	DCA	BOS	1114	1217	1:03	
387	BOS	STL	1525	1659	2:34	
387	STL	IAH	1742	1931	1:49	7/4/77
559	IAH	SAT	2100	2140	:40	
559	SAT	ELP	2210	2222	1:12	
496	ELP	SAT	0205	0419	1:14	
496	SAT	IAH	0445	0528	:43	7/6/77
642	IAH	STL	0820	1002	1:42	
642	STL	BOS	1025	1344	2:19	
551	BOS	DCA	1000	1116	1:16	
551	DCA	CVG	1200	1318	1:18	7/10/77
406	CVG	ORD	1400	1554	:54	

(Then deadheaded ORD to DFW)

568	DFW	BNA	1550	1725	1:35	
568	BNA	DCA	1750	2022	1:32	7/11/77
568	DCA	BOS	2100	2212	1:12	

THE NEW AIRLINER CAPTAIN OF TODAY

Flight No.	From	To	Depart	Arrive	Time	Date
465	BOS	ORD	1320	1449	2:29	
106	ORD	YYZ	1645	1907	1:22	7/13/77
224	YYZ	EWR	1900	2120	1:20	
249	LGA	DFW	1440	1650	3:10	7/14/77
286	DFW	BOS	1900	2335	3:35	
415	BOS	DTW	0745	0923	1:38	
415	DTW	ORD	1020	1018	:58	7/18/77
427	ORD	SAT	1250	1515	2:25	
482	SAT	ORD	0700	0923	2:23	
482	ORD	DCA	1000	1227	1:27	7/19/77
482	DCA	BOS	1310	1424	1:14	
465	BOS	ORD	1320	1446	2:26	
106	ORD	YYZ	1649	1908	1:19	7/24/77
224	YYZ	EWR	2000	2111	1:11	
85	LGA	DFW	1215	1425	3:10	7/25/77
286	DFW	BOS	1921	2337	3:16	

These listings were taken from Captain Felder's own log. The hours of departure and arrival are for the time zone in which the cities are located. The figures listed under "Time" are for the elapsed flight time. Some schedules also take the captain to Indianapolis, Memphis and Rochester, N. Y.

To ever have a chance to captain a 747, Felder would have

to transfer to a larger base, such as New York, from which these aircraft are flown. He also would need much greater seniority rank than he feels he'll ever possess, considering his age and relatively late advancement to pilot.

Still, he has 20 years yet before mandatory retirement. Many of the veteran pilots are now reaching the end of the line, and the airline industry anticipates marked expansion of business in forthcoming years.

"I'll just wait and see what occurs, and what I can do," says Felder.

Felder and the former N. Drue Cox of West Palm Beach, Florida, were married just before his first Navy assignment. She had some difficulty adjusting to Navy life, Felder says, but managed. Even so, she was never totally at ease.

"When I took her to Pensacola as a bride, just about the first thing to happen was a student crashing in an F9F Panther, the plane I was then flying. The investigators said he crashed because of low blood sugar resulting from lack of breakfast. Drue always got up with me and fixed breakfast whatever time I had to fly from then on.

"Drue worries some, I guess, but she keeps most of it to herself. She's been a very good pilot's wife. Always smoothing over arguments before I fly, never being demanding when I have to work. She knows I live in two worlds and she's only in one of them.

"Airline pilots, I understand, have a bad success rate with wives. Drue and I have problems as everyone else does. But so far we've been able to talk them out.

"I believe Drue likes my profession, even with the loneliness it brings her, because of the money, the days off, and travel, and because it keeps me happy."

Captain and Mrs. Felder have two daughters, Tara, 18, and Martha, 16. Both want to take flying lessons and Tara has expressed some interest in the possibility of a flying career. For a long while Martha has thought she would like to be a stewardess.

"I do not try to lead them into anything," says Felder, "but encourage them in whatever direction they take.

"Tara's eyes are correctable, but not good. That may make it hard. However, I will not be the one to say she cannot fly a plane for a living. She has only recently become interested in aviation and we have not discussed it much."

Looking back on his own experiences, Captain Felder has this advice for young people interested in pursuing an airline-pilot career: "You have to get your degree and I think it would be better if it were in mathematics or engineering. It's not really necessary to know a lot of numbers, though, because you don't sit there and count things and consider the stresses on the rivets. You have to pay attention to other things.

"You have to be rather analytical about things and not really quick to act because you certainly don't want to do the wrong thing. Be deliberate and steady, that sort of thing. Pilots are careful to follow the rules. We are very conservative—or else!"

As for training in the beginning: "The military has a warm place for me because it gave me my start. I recommend the military because, let's face it, they fly very modern

AIRLINE PILOT

airplanes. They're the latest equipment. Their procedures are very refined.

"The military has a way of condensing it all and giving it to you in a hurry, though it's not to say you can't do it another way and be just as good a pilot."

To Felder, nothing could come near matching flying as a career.

"I'd do it for less pay. But the pay is great. I enjoy flying . . . the work itself, the airplane, the people you meet, the problems you encounter. Sometimes it's like a piece of cake and sometimes you earn your pay . . ."

Long ago someone came up with the wry statement, still often quoted to budding airline pilots by old-timers, that "flying is hours of boredom interspersed with a few moments of sheer terror."

Captain Felder is not one ever terrorized a whit.

"I can't think of anything I don't like about it. There are things we complain about at times but they're just piddling little things.

"I enjoy it all. I can't think of anything I'd rather do than what I'm doing." With a smile he added, "I have always liked myself better when either flying or talking about flying."

11

Flying Around the World

It was a case of true love at first sight—with an airplane—for Douglas Moody. The romance with flying that resulted has lasted nearly 40 years. During that time Moody was to become one of the key pilots in making Pan American World Airways what it is today.

Back in 1937 or 1938 Moody, who was around 19 at the time, was a student at the University of California, Berkeley. He was living at home in San Mateo and driving back and forth to classes. Every day he passed a little airport, then known as Mills Field and the forerunner of what has become San Francisco International Airport.

"One day I saw this beautiful little low-winged airplane sitting there," Moody reminisces. "I thought I just *had* to fly that thing. But those were tough times. None of us had much money, if any.

"But I went in and talked to the fellow who owned it. He said he had hocked his soul to buy that plane and another, a Piper Cub. He said, 'We're going to have a flying club here and you gotta give me $25.' Then there was to be so much an hour for flying. I forget what, but I think it was $6 an hour for the cub and $14 for the other, which was a Ryan ST. It was built by the same company that had built Lindbergh's *Spirit of St. Louis.*

"I don't know how I paid for things. Might have sold a couple of suits to Jake, the old-clothes man at college, or some such. Anyway I got up enough money."

Before that, Moody had never had the slightest inclination to take up flying, or even thought of it.

"Just seeing that plane triggered it, I believe. And the fact that there I was at the university and really didn't have any idea what the hell I wanted to do. I was in engineering college for a year and my adviser told me that if I wanted to stay in college I'd better get out of that."

Moody had been in a plane only once before in his life. He had previously attended the Hill School at Pottstown, Pennsylvania, and flew home in a DC-2 or DC-3 after his last year there. In those days a transcontinental trip took 12 hours or more. Many of the planes had berths in them. It was in one of these that Moody had flown. However, the trip didn't give rise to any thoughts of becoming a pilot. It took that Ryan ST to capture Moody's fancy.

"I got started, and the law then was that you could solo at the end of eight hours. I had just enough money to get through the solo thing. I had a couple of hours in the Cub and the rest in the Ryan.

"One morning about dawn, when there wasn't any wind or anything, the owner was crazy enough to let me take the Ryan around the field once. That was my solo flight. I felt like a real big shot."

Captain Douglas Moody—globe girdler. (Pan American World Airways)

After all his years as a pilot, flying almost everything up to the largest and fastest airliners, Moody is still in love with the Ryan.

"It was a beautiful airplane. There are still a few of them left. You see them around at air shows. Some fellows have restored them to their original glory. That plane was far ahead of its time."

In the summer of 1939 Moody went to Europe on a vacation trip. While in Munich he saw a show of German aircraft and was much impressed by the technological advances which the Nazis had made. He also became convinced that war was imminent, as did some friends who were on the trip with him.

"A couple of us tried to stay in England and join an 'Eagle Squadron' or something. Of course we had no qualifications at the time. We were also too young and they threw us out."

In time, Moody was to get his wartime flying service, however. As it turned out, he was destined to become an airline pilot first.

Moody was in the Naval Reserve Officers' Training Corps at Berkeley. When he got home he headed for the Boeing School of Aeronautics at nearby Oakland Airport and enrolled. This was the only school of its kind at the time. It had an accelerated flight training course with instruction in such advanced flying techniques as instrument navigation. It also had Link Trainers, an early version of today's cockpit simulators.

The school had been established by United Airlines and the Boeing Aircraft Manufacturing Company, and was operated jointly by them. All the instructors were United captains.

Moody says the captains were rough taskmasters indeed. But since it wasn't easy for him or his fellow students to get a job at anything else in those times, they "shaped up and worked hard." That hard work produced some of the world's finest airline pilots in the years to come.

The basic trainer was a Boeing 203, a heavy biplane with two open cockpits, one behind the other, which had been used in military services. Also in use was a Boeing 40. This was an old airmail plane, one of the nation's first, and it had been rigged up for instrument flying. Moody also learned to fly DC-3s, then the "modern" thing on airlines, and Boeing 247s which had preceded them.

As graduation time at the Boeing school approached Moody was accepted by United Airlines. He applied for a job on the east coast but was assigned to what he regarded as the "Rockpile Run"—Seattle to Salt Lake City "over the rocks," or Rocky Mountains. Moody wasn't overly entranced by the prospect.

Meanwhile one of his fellow pilots had paid a visit to a Pan American base, located on Treasure Island in the San Francisco Bay, and was well received there. He told Moody about it. Moody sneaked off from training one day and visited Pan Am too. He also got a warm reception and an indication Pan Am was interested in him.

"The big glamor of flying internationally hit me, rather than going to Seattle to Chicago or some jerky stuff like that. I could think of nothing but flying a glamorous boat to Rio or across the Pacific. Those flights were just starting."

Somehow word of Moody's hookey visit to Pan Am leaked to United's people at the school. Moody was called in and told to make up his mind either to stay or to go. Moody said he didn't know whether Pan American actually would take him.

"My chief instructor sent me in to see his boss and the boss said, 'If you want to go with them, you go over there, and if they'll take you, fine. If not you can come back here and you've got a job.' I almost broke into tears. That was the nicest thing in the world.

"Pan American did accept me. That was thirty-seven and a half years ago, so obviously I've been happy here, and more or less successful."

He has also had a warm spot in his heart for United Airlines ever after, too.

Moody had a couple of unusual experiences on his first checkout with Pan American.

"We were given a flight test in a big two-engine Consolidated Commodore flying boat. I didn't know which end was up in a boat. I'd never been in one in my life and I did a perfectly terrible job in the thing. The guy that was with me did so much better, but they didn't take him.

"I thought they had made a mistake. But apparently this fellow had been a copilot with another airline and they didn't think he did as well. In other words I think they wanted a guy with no habits, or no bad habits, or somebody that didn't know anything and that's what they got with me.

"They were terribly polite in those days. Believe it or not, we were even asked where we would like to go and I said I would like to go to Rio. They had a little base down there."

Moody was told to report to Miami, Florida, which was the takeoff point for Caribbean flights. He and another young pilot decided to drive there and, being at the carefree age, have fun along the way. Among other things, they stopped for the Mardi Gras in New Orleans.

The trip took them two months. "We didn't know about seniority or any of that stuff in those days, so we lost a whole bunch of numbers." Seniority began only after they signed on at an operating base. In the meantime others had gotten ahead of them in seniority by arriving a few days earlier.

Moody and his pal were in for an icy reception when they finally ambled into Miami.

"The chief pilot there looked at me and says, 'Who the hell are you?' I said, 'I'm Moody. I'm here to go to Rio.' 'Oh,' he says, '*really?*' He had a good-looking red-haired secretary and he said, 'Kay, get this guy a time card and tell him where to go to get the overalls. He can go to work in the hangar tomorrow.' He was muttering, 'Jesus, I don't know where they hire these guys.'

"Well, I went right smack into the hangar and I worked there three months. We had to get an A&E license in those days—an aircraft and engines license. As a copilot on a two-engine boat, if anything broke down the copilot was supposed to be able to fix it. They said they didn't want those captains who were getting paid six hundred dollars a month to hurt themselves doing it. They didn't care if we fell off the wing or anything like that. I was getting only two hundred dollars.

"But I had to do only one job in my whole career, I think. I had to change a cylinder once and it took me forever. That was down in Cuba. It was hot and my tools kept falling in the water. The captain was sitting on the porch of this old hotel drinking rum swizzles."

Pan American eventually gave Moody training on various

types of flying boats and amphibians with wheels removed. His first command came later on the four-engine Sikorsky 42, the flagship of the fleet.

Flying the Caribbean in those days was a matter of island-hopping, down as far as Rio de Janeiro. Moody had finally made it.

All the flying was done in the daytime with stopovers along the way at night. "It was wonderful flying," Moody recalls—with occasional extra enjoyment when the captain had a whim to see some new place not on the airline route.

"The captain was God in those days. When he left Miami and wanted to overnight in some island he hadn't been to, he did. He'd just decide that the plane had developed a little problem and head for that island. If you tried that now, they'd send a guy in a white coat with a net to get you."

During the first part of World War II Moody remained, technically, with Pan American but was assigned to fly planes for the naval air transport service between the states and Alaska as well as in Alaska. Part of the time he was pilot for an admiral stationed at Dutch Harbor. Many flights were for returning ill service men to the states.

Subsequently Moody was transferred to New York, where he flew the Atlantic, bringing home war casualties from Europe, and then to Miami for similar flights to and from Africa. By then the C-54 had been developed. This was a four-engine aircraft which became the DC-4 after the war and replaced the DC-3.

Once the war was over it was back to the DC-3 and the Caribbean for Moody, however, for a time while the C-54s were being converted for airline operation. A more advanced plane was being readied, though, and soon was in service. It was the four-engine Constellation and it served as Pan American's workhorse for many years.

As the years rolled by, new planes made their debut in kaleidoscopic fashion: the DC-6 and DC-7, the Boeing Stratocruiser, the first jet—the B-707—and then the DC-8 and B-747. Moody flew all of them.

Meanwhile, Pan American was expanding routes around the globe and Moody was in the midst of it all. By now he was back in New York and helping establish many of the new routes as well as flying them in regular service. He has flown around the world many times.

Moody was one of the first pilots to fly the huge 747. He and five other senior pilots were sent to Seattle where the 747s were being built.

"We were in the test program and acceptance of the plane. My boss and I delivered the first one to the company."

Of all the planes he has ever flown, Moody regards the 747 as the most enjoyable to handle. But he says it is really more a matter of management than flying.

"The crew sits there and monitors the systems that are working on the thing. The redundancy there is fantastic." "Redundancy" denotes backup systems for anything that goes wrong. The 747 has as many as five systems for operating some of its equipment. "It lands like a big Piper Cub. It's honest. It's just beautiful."

Requirements for pilots flying international routes for the major airlines are generally the same as for those in domestic service, with a couple of exceptions.

AIRLINE PILOT

Pan American requires that all pilots have navigation training. While aircraft flying the oceans are guided by inertial navigation systems, the airline wants everyone in the cockpit to be able if necessary to do it the old-fashioned way. That's by shooting the sun or stars with a sextant.

Also, international pilots fly somewhat more than others. The maximum is 255 hours per quarter. This works out to 85 hours a month but pilot time isn't restricted to a monthly basis.

"Pilots are allowed to go over that if they are 'down line disrupted,'" Moody explains. "In other words if a fellow is in Frankfurt and thinks he's coming back, but we have to send him to Tehran or somewhere else, and he's going to go over his time, that would be credited to the next month.

"You can't put any lid on it and have any flexibility. We must have some flexibility because of the nature of the routes and distances flown."

Normally a pilot will fly halfway around the world, either from the east or west coast, and then return over the same route. The meeting point is either New Delhi, India, or Bangkok, Thailand. A pilot will have rest layovers at various points along either route, and will be gone from home several days at a time. The layovers are no longer the fun they once were.

"When we used to have two or three days at some places we had a good time—played golf, had lots of parties, anything the traffic would bear. Besides that, everybody was younger. Now the layovers are so short and everybody's so tired you don't do anything much but sleep and get up and go back to work."

Everyone has heard of the time-lag problem and it is a real

consideration in international flying too, especially on the long runs. Moody says pilots have tried all kinds of remedies but nothing seems to work particularly well.

Moody makes about four round trips a month to London and Amsterdam, but spends a great deal of additional time flying abroad as a check pilot with new men and as an instructor at the line's training base at Kennedy Airport in New York.

Asked how many miles he had flown in his career, Moody had to take time out and calculate a while. He finally figured that it had to be at least 6 million miles or more. He has spent around 30,000 hours in the air as a pilot.

For some years the captain was assigned to the White House by Pan American. He flew the press plane, which was operated by Pan Am, in the Kennedy-Johnson era and made one trip after Richard Nixon became president.

He made one round-the-world trip with President Johnson. He is not about to forget his press flights with Johnson. In that president's entourage everyone had to be ready to move at a moment's notice. Johnson would decide to get going at odd times, and could be extremely snappish over any delay. Kennedy's schedules were spelled out long in advance.

Through all the years of flying Moody says he had only one emergency of any kind.

"It was a runaway propeller on a Stratocruiser. It happened to me over Nantucket and I had to land at Boston on a bad snowy night. Runaway propellers were a common thing at the time, but I couldn't feather it. It was shaking the wing very badly.

"But we managed to get it stopped without the engine

AIRLINE PILOT

catching on fire. We froze it—cut the oil off to make the engine stop."

What has Moody liked best about his career?

The change of scenery all the time. . . . new planes and equipment developed through the years. . . . new routes to fly. . . . the "more than generous time off". . . . the pay. . . . pleasant people met and good friends made. . . . the type of personnel in the airline business—"they're top-drawer."

There has been little or nothing he hasn't liked. He says the only things that might be considered negatives are odd-hour flying schedules or unexpected schedule changes, working on weekends and being away from home for extended periods.

"But I consider these things more an inconvenience than anything else. In any business you have to have your share of that."

What was his oddest experience?

"I don't know. Maybe it's that I'm the only guy who has never seen a UFO."

As for advice to young people, Moody thinks it would be well for them to have more of a mechanical and engineering background than he did. They should complete college, too.

"Flying is going to be more and more technical. That old seat-of-the-pants-flying stuff has gone out the window. Young people also are going to have a tremendous opportunity going into this space shuttle thing."

Moody and his wife live in Darien, Connecticut. They have three children, two girls and a boy, all grown. For a while the boy had an interest in flying but had to give it up because of an eye problem. Moody says he never pushed it with his children, anyway.

In his time off Moody likes to play golf—and fly. He doesn't have a plane of his own but goes to an airport at nearby Bridgeport and takes up single-engine aircraft available there.

Just for fun.

12

After Making Captain, What?

There are many unusual aspects to the life of a senior captain for a major airline.

However, no one should be surprised to learn that his pay puts him in a class with corporate executives. At mid-1977 the top scale was around $100,000 a year with fringe benefits. No women had yet reached this level, but it seems assured some will in the future.

A captain's rate of pay is based on four things: seniority, the type of plane, the route flown, and whether the flying is done during the daytime or at night.

Income is much higher for those who fly the fastest and heaviest aircraft, and for those on international schedules or whose trips are primarily over water. Night flying draws a somewhat higher scale, though the extra income is not so great as in the other cases.

A pilot's base pay increases each year for the first 12 years he is a captain but not thereafter. In other words, a 12-year man flying a DC-10 will receive the same as a 14-year man flying the same equipment.

AFTER MAKING CAPTAIN, WHAT?

Generally speaking, the top earners are those flying 747s on international or Caribbean routes. However, trips to Canada or Mexico are not considered international routes by some airlines.

Seniority plays an important part in what a captain ultimately earns. As it increases it affords a pilot the opportunity to advance to larger planes and to bid on the most lucrative flight schedules.

What may come as a surprise to many people is that captains get paid for overtime, too, if they should incur it. Not only that, but they receive commensurate time off as well.

While most of the leading airline labor contracts restrict pilots to 75 hours flying time a month, there are instances when, by necessity, they will exceed it. They could be delayed on particular flights by weather or mechanical troubles, for instance. Or in waiting to land when an airport has a jam-up of incoming traffic.

In addition to the overtime pay, the extra flying time at some airlines is in effect in a "time bank." It works the same way as a savings account. When a pilot has accumulated enough time in the account, he or she one day will call the line and say, "I have eleven and a half hours in the bank, so I'm going to drop my last trip of the month."

Some things vary from airline to airline, for both captain and cockpit crew, but in major respects they are identical either because of FAA regulations or pilot union contracts. Most pilots are members of the Air Line Pilots Association or Allied Pilots Association, both of which have provided strong representation for many years.

Examples of operating conditions covered here are based on those in effect with one of the nation's leading airlines. Many of the rules and amenities apply to copilots and flight engineers as well, but the discussion here will be limited to captains. And before anyone starts taking things amiss, it should be said that the term "he" applies equally to both men and women.

As far as work is concerned, the captain has a great many choices to make. Life can be quite varied if desired.

All airlines have what are designated as "bases." These are major cities which are pivotal to flight operations. Each captain works from a particular base.

A captain will put in only 12 or 13 actual working days a month. The number depends on what schedules are flown and how much flying time they involve. A captain's flying time generally is limited to 8 hours a day, though overall duty time can be considerably longer.

Each airline base has numerous flights out daily, of varying lengths, stops en route and destinations. Every month, around the 20th, each captain bids on whatever schedules of flights he desires for the next month.

Generally, he'll get his wishes. An exception would be if someone with greater seniority bid on the same thing. In that case, he will receive his next choice provided he has the seniority to "hold" that bid. In other words, he may bid as many trip selections as he wants, and where he falls in the seniority list determines what bid he will be awarded.

In any event, the airline will notify the captain by about the 25th of the month what his next month's flight duties will be.

AFTER MAKING CAPTAIN, WHAT?

This enables a captain to know in advance what his days off will be. Thus he can make plans to go fishing, skiing, take his family on a trip or tend to outside interests he may have.

Sometimes a captain will have two days off between flights. At other times there could be three or four. Under the union contract the airline is obligated to arrange a specified number of two-day off-work periods each month.

The time off between trips also is partially determined by the way a work schedule is set up. A run might involve flights to different cities around the country, over a three-day period, before the captain returns to base. In such a case he then would have four days off before the next flight. Here is an example of a three-day flight schedule:

First day: Boston, New York, Washington, Nashville, Memphis, Little Rock and Dallas. Overnight in Dallas.

Second Day: Dallas, New York, Boston, Chicago. Overnight in Chicago.

Third Day: Chicago, New York, Chicago, New York. Home.

Some pilots prefer making basically the same runs and will bid them month after month. Others enjoy varying their activity.

The bidding process, occurring so often, is a highly complex and expensive operation for a large airline. While it is now done with a central computer, a huge administrative staff is needed to sort out the bids and program the computer. A big airline may have 4,000 pilots or more, and 1,000 or more flight departures a day.

In one respect, a captain's job is just like anyone else's: he has to travel to and from home at his own expense. After that, though, many things are markedly different.

When a captain reaches his destination for the day he is provided limousine service to and from a motel or hotel, if he has to remain overnight between flights. He has a meal allowance. The airline pays all costs. In flight, of course, he also is provided with his meals.

Although a captain's scheduled flying time is limited to 8 hours per working day, it could be exceeded if there were a delay of some kind while aloft. In that case, the captain continues to the destination. After all, he can't very well walk off the job when time is up.

If for some reason a flight should be terminated at a city other than the scheduled destination, the captain's lodging, food and limousine expenses are borne by the company.

A captain can be scheduled for up to 14 hours of duty during a working day. The extra time covers activities related to a flight schedule. For example, the captain must be at the airport of departure an hour before takeoff. This time is devoted to checking out the plane and making other preparations for flight.

Other working time may be spent on the ground during stopovers on a route. In the event that a mechanical problem or other matter happened to delay the captain so that the 14-hour limit would be exceeded, it would be illegal under FAA rules for him to continue.

A substitute captain would be called in to continue the trip, while the original captain would be given appropriate rest before making another flight. The next day he might be assigned to some other schedule or returned home as a passenger.

AFTER MAKING CAPTAIN, WHAT?

Similarly, a captain wouldn't be allowed to take off on a flight if it were to carry him beyond his 8-hour limit.

There can be what is called a "field break" between flights. A captain might be scheduled to shift from one plane to another at some point, with 4 hours or more between flights. During such a period the company would put him up at a motel near the airport or send him to a downtown hotel. Normally, however, the minimum rest time between schedules is 8 to 10 hours.

An oddity is that a few captains live nowhere near the bases they operate from. And they fly to work.

This kind of thing occurs when, say, a captain is based in Chicago and lives at Dallas. If he has a morning flight out of Chicago he'll fly there the night before and spend the night at his own expense.

Almost everything goes by seniority. Pilots can change bases of operations if there is an opening for a captain at another and they have the rank to make the winning bid. If a captain retires or otherwise leaves the service at San Francisco, for instance, the company will send notices to all other bases such as "October—One captain bid open in San Francisco." Anyone wishing to transfer there sends in his name and employee number. Whoever has the highest seniority gets the position. Once there, he bids on certain runs as before.

If the captain should not happen to be qualified to fly the type of aircraft operating out of the new base he will be sent to train for it.

When a captain is transferred at his own request he must pay his own moving expenses. Sometimes the company will order a transfer. In that case the company pays the expenses.

A captain may be called upon during days off to fill in when there is an emergency need for his services. This could result from many of the things mentioned heretofore—regular pilots reaching their work-day or flight-time limits. But a fill-in pilot must be qualified to fly the type of aircraft being used.

Sometimes the substitute is what is called a "management pilot." There is at least one such person at every base. Their administrative duties are to keep flight operations going smoothly. Some fly regular schedules a part of the month. Some spend almost all their time with administrative duties. All are senior captains.

One in New York says that on several occasions he has had to climb into a cockpit and take over, attired in a business suit rather than uniform, because the regular pilot had called in to say he was stuck in traffic or couldn't make it for some other reason.

Other bits and pieces about a pilot's professional life and times:

Long ago, when a pilot was assigned to a run which required landing at an airport he'd never seen, instructors would take him on a practice run. Now he familiarizes himself with a new airport, its runways and environs by videotape. This is mandatory.

If you observe a captain approaching or leaving his plane, you will notice that he carries a special kind of case in addition to any personal luggage. The special bag contains

AFTER MAKING CAPTAIN, WHAT?

maps of the entire airline system. These are for use if he should have to change to unfamiliar routes for any reason, such as weather conditions.

The captain's case also will contain what are called "approach plates." They are for various airports. They describe individual airports and the visual and instrument procedures for each. These are necessary when a pilot has to divert from his scheduled airport, because of fog or other conditions, to another that is unfamiliar to him.

Captains get vacations like anyone else too. The maximum is 5 weeks after 25 years of service.

Pilots buy their own uniforms.

Pensions are substantial. There is a fixed-income benefit plus a variable annuity type plan which takes into account changes in the cost of living.

If there is any overall testimonial to the safety of modern airliners and the men who fly them, it surely must be this: captains pay the same rate for life insurance as everybody else.

13

Takeoff to Tomorrow

A glowing future seems in prospect for the U.S. airline industry, in both domestic and foreign service.

Experts who have taken a long look ahead can see nothing but continued growth until at least the year 2000.

Some truly stunning forecasts come from the Air Transport Association of America. This organization represents nearly all of the nation's scheduled airlines. In a mid-1977 report to the National Transportation Policy Study Commission, the association made these predictions:

- Domestic airline revenue passenger-miles—the number of miles flown by paying passengers—are expected to nearly double between 1974 and 1987 and to triple by 1995. At the same time, the average *annual growth* in the mid-1990s should equal the *total* industry revenue passenger-miles of an *entire* year in the mid-1950s.

- Annual aircraft movements are expected to increase from 8 million in 1974 to nearly 15 million in the year 2000.

- Domestic passenger growth—the total of passengers

carried by the airlines—could nearly triple to more than 600 million by the end of the century.

• International passenger traffic is expected to increase even more than in domestic service. The average annual growth is projected at one percent above domestic travel—or more than six percent annually—until the 1990s.

• Between 1976 and 1989 the nation's airline industry expects to spend $65 billion for new equipment. About half will be for equipment to replace present aircraft and the remainder will provide for traffic growth.

There are many reasons for these forecasts. The world population is still growing. More people have money to spend on personal travel. Business and industry are expanding, domestically and internationally, necessitating more employee travel. Other modes of travel do not offer the conveniences and speed over long distances.

There are other considerations. Automobiles are becoming increasingly expensive to acquire and operate. Fuel costs may well skyrocket in the near future. Existing roads and highways are suffering growing traffic density and delays, as well as becoming more hazardous. It does not appear probable that there will be significant highway construction or upgrading in the foreseeable future.

At times during the past several years economic conditions put a crimp in the phenomenal growth of the airline industry. As of mid-1977, however, all indications were that the forward movement had been resumed. Many pilots, who had been furloughed for months or years, were being called back to service and new ones hired for training.

In 1976 the airlines carried 223 million passengers. That

was 18 million more than in the previous year and 105 million more than 10 years previously. This was 80 percent of all intercity passenger travel-miles by public carrier. Four of every five first-class letters moved by air.

The airlines were operating nearly 2,300 aircraft on 13,000 daily flights, carrying more than 600,000 passengers a day in domestic and international service along with 9,000 tons of freight and 2,500 tons of mail.

If, as a young man or woman, you begin preparing now, what kind of aircraft will you fly when you make captain? Supersonic jets? Hypersonic jets? Hydrogen-powered aircraft? Rocket ships?

Perhaps, but not likely. Chances are it will be a plane closely resembling those in service now. Changes now foreseen by the experts will be evolutionary rather than revolutionary in commercial aviation aircraft.

Changes will come in technology: more fuel-efficient planes, all-weather landing devices to eliminate delays, and engines redesigned to reduce or eliminate noise and environmental harm.

The trend toward greater computerization of airplane operational equipment will continue. But even as technological sophistication of aircraft advances, people still will have to fly the planes. They will need more knowledge and skill than now.

The economics of airline operation are such that planes in use during the next few years won't be markedly different from the subsonic and narrow-body jets flown today. In fact, it is the 727 that has become the modern-day workhorse and promises to continue as such for years to come. There are far more of these craft on order from the manufacturers for the future than anything else. Combined orders for the 747, DC-9 and DC-10 are in a distant second place.

Much of the industry effort now is devoted to planning planes tailored for greater and less expensive mass transportation—more seats and fewer galleys, and bargain-price, no-frills service.

This isn't to say that the supersonic transport, such as now represented by the controversial British-French Concorde, doesn't have any prospect for the future.

Some industry sources believe there eventually will be a substantial demand for the high-speed service provided by this type of aircraft. This will come primarily from business concerns which value time saving in travel. And there will always be others who simply want to get from one place to another as fast as possible despite the premium fare.

As of now the SST is hampered by high fuel costs and environmental problems. These in time probably can be overcome through engineering developments. Nevertheless, no sizable SST usage is envisioned until the 1990s or the 21st century, if at all.

A fair number of design engineers think the SST will be bypassed for a hypersonic transport (HST). This type of craft would make the run from New York to Paris in less than 2 hours, possibly, at speeds of 3,000 to 4,000 miles per hour. There are a few others who envision rocket ship flights from New York to Tokyo in 90 minutes.

A far more distant prospect—or maybe not so distant, either—is the use of hydrogen for aircraft propulsion. A major question today is how long the world's fossil fuel supply will last, or under what conditions it will be obtainable, since the United States has become increasingly dependent on foreign sources.

The foremost attribute of hydrogen is that it can be produced from water in vast quantities since the water supply is virtually limitless. Even so, there is a heated debate over the economic feasibility. Some engineers maintain that it takes eight times as much energy to separate hydrogen from water molecules as the energy that would be provided. Others dispute this.

Whatever the case may be, there is no question that enormous expenditures would be necessary for huge-scale hydrogen production and aircraft usage.

While no great changes may be in the offing for the next decade or more, tomorrow's airliner captains might well find some interesting and exciting changes before they conclude their careers.

One question that is giving rise to more and more thought in airline executive offices is this: where are tomorrow's pilots going to get the training and experience that qualify them for airline acceptance?

While there is an ample backlog of superbly skilled people available for the immediate future, it won't last forever.

The supply is expected to dwindle because, for one thing, the military services are training far fewer people than in past years. Meanwhile many of the old pros like Russell Sapp and Douglas Moody will be reaching retirement age. Others will be lost through physical disabilities, death and for other reasons.

If airline growth equals the predictions, the need for more pilots is going to be extensive. There is a possibility that shortages could develop within a decade. If so, what can be done?

Richard L. Spaulding, vice president of Allegheny Airlines, has concluded that there is only one answer. The airlines will have to do what they did in the beginning—provide much or most of the pilot training themselves.

Spaulding sees this as a real possibility within 10 years. If the necessity does arise, he believes the airlines will undertake a joint enterprise to provide the training, rather than try to do it separately. A flight training academy would be established under sponsorship of the airlines and the airline association, and probably with some government funding.

"All the airlines would contribute and all could draw from this source," Spaulding says. "I don't know any other way because there's certainly no easy way that a young person can afford this kind of training.

"Once you get out of the light airplane, where do you go to get the experience with the multiengine heavy equipment? It's difficult, even now."

One way to regard the possibility of preparing for a pilot's job with an airline, no matter how it is approached, is to compare the process with that necessary to become a doctor, lawyer or any other exceptionally skilled professional.

For the most part, things are very much the same. All take time, money, patience and dedication. All require higher education plus specialized training. In any of them it is well to begin laying the foundation as early as possible. Even in junior high school.

AIRLINE PILOT

There are two chief differences between aviation and the other careers. One is that upon completion of educational requirements a doctor or lawyer, for instance, can begin work immediately. For a pilot aspiring to the top rank things are much more uncertain. There is no guarantee of ever attaining the ultimate.

Another consideration is that almost any other professional may pursue his or her work with physical disabilities, even if they developed before, during or after the preparatory work. A pilot cannot.

The pilot who makes it, however, can look to a monetary reward comparable to that of many of the highest-pay professions. Only at the very beginning will it be rather modest.

The pilot starting as a second officer, or flight engineer, receives approximately $12,000 a year. That does not include fringe benefits, which are considerable. A second officer's pay may go as high as $46,000 a year.

Once the copilot status is reached the base pay can go up to $53,000 a year, not including other benefits. Base pilot pay ranges up to $80,000 annually.

Upon retirement an $80,000-a-year captain will receive a pension of approximately $40,000. Along with it will be an airline pass. At 60 there should be plenty of time to do other things if desired, or just relax and take it easy.

Another aspect of a flying career that should not be overlooked is that if one should fail to make it to the pinnacle with a major airline, there are many other piloting or administrative positions. Many of these are financially and professionally satisfying, whether with a top-rank carrier or other organization.

TAKEOFF TO TOMORROW

If you are a young man or woman who feels a genuine urge to take up flying, you would be wise to give it a try. Take a few beginning lessons on a small aircraft. By the time you've reached the solo stage, you should know whether you're suited for it, and it for you.

There will be much, much more to do and learn before you get to the controls of a 747. It won't always be easy.

Anyway, you know what it takes. If you still feel an overwhelming desire, get started. Now.

You are cleared for takeoff.

A Note of Thanks

This book would not have been possible without a great many exceptional people who took time out from their busy professional or personal lives to assist me in every way possible. To all of them I want to express, once again, my utmost thanks and gratitude.

Some are quoted in the text. Others include:

Mr. David C. Frailey, Vice President—Public Relations, American Airlines, New York.

Major Ralph R. Williams, Office of Information, The Air Force, New York.

Mr. C. Bruce Plowman, Director—Publicity, Continental Airlines, Los Angeles.

Mr. Paul Friend, Public Relations Manager, Pan American World Airways, New York.

Ms. Mary Budke, Public Relations Representative, Frontier Airlines, Denver, Colorado.

Mr. Daniel Z. Henkin, Vice President—Public Relations, Air Transport Association of America, Washington, D.C.

Captain D. E. Ehmann, Vice President—Flight, American Airlines, Fort Worth, Texas.

Mr. Jessel V. Williams, Federal Aviation Administration, Euless, Texas.

Mr. Robert R. Mozdean, Administrator, Selection Programs, and Ms. Donna M. Dorn, Manager—Selection, American Airlines, New York.

At the American Airlines Flight Academy, Fort Worth, Texas: Mr. R. L. Bisbee, Director—Ground School Instruction; Captain A. M. Reeser, Assistant Vice President, Flying—Technical; Dr. Robert C. Houston, Director, Training Support; Mr. David C. Killian, Manager, Audio Visual Center; Mr. Robert J. Kalina, Supervisor, B-707 Flying Training Ground School; and Captain H. B. Benninghoff, Assistant Vice President, Flying.

Capt. John J. Kenny, Flight Superintendent, American Airlines, New York.

* * *

I'd like to convey very special thanks to Mr. Larry Strain, the American Airlines Public Relations Director for Operations, New York.

He devoted an extraordinary amount of time to arranging interviews and other research activities. He also personally provided much material relating to airlines' operations as well as flying in general.

Still further, he served as an editorial backstop in reviewing my manuscript for accuracy.

* * *

And special thanks also to my wife, Joy, for putting her own good editorial eye to my work once more.

FRANK STILLEY

Index

Air Force
  officer training, 33
  pilot instructors, 37–38
  pilot training, 14–15, 17, 32–45
  pilot training bases, 33–34
  qualifications, 33
  silver wings, 38
  women, 15, 44–45, 75–86
Air Force Academy, 33, 45
Air Force Pilot Instructor Training School, 37
Air Force Reserve, 38, 76
Air Force Reserve Officers' Training Corps, 33
Airline captains
  pensions, 131
  salaries, 124–25
  schedules, 126–30
  vacations, 131
Airline flight schools, 57–65
Airline industry
  future of, 132–37
Airline pilots
  careers for, 9–15
  employment for, 50–51
  future for, 136–37
  preparing for careers for, 12–13, 17–31, 137–38
  qualifications for, 12, 17–18, 46–51, 55
  retirement for, 104, 138
  salaries for, 138
  screening for, 52–56
  seniority for, 55
  training programs for, 57–65
Air Line Pilots Association, 73, 125
Airplanes
  Boeing 40, 115
  Boeing 203, 115
  C-54, 118
  C-9, 76
  C-141 Starlifter, 76
  Constellation, 119
  DC-3, 87
  Hercules turboprop C-130, 42
  B-747, 119
  KC-135, 76
  Ryan ST, 112
  T-38 Talon, 36–37, 40
  T-37, 36
Air Training Command, 33
Air Transport Association of America, 132
Allied Pilots Association, 125
Amelia Earhart Award, 73
American Airlines, 49, 57–58, 63, 65, 90
  qualifications for employment at, 49–51
Approach plates, 131
Army
  air training program, 41–42

AIRLINE PILOT

helicopter pilots, 41–42
Army Air Corps, 90
Aviation Daily, 67

Basic maneuvers, 22
Bidding process, 127, 128
Boeing Aircraft Manufacturing Company, 114
Boeing School of Aeronautics, 114

Clinton Aviation Company, 73
Cockpit Procedures Training (CPT), 61
Columbus Air Force Base, 33
Continental Airlines, 67, 68, 70
Crawford, Victoria K., 84
Cross-country flying, 23, 24, 36

Department of Transportation, 19
Donahue, Mary E., 84
Drugs, 12, 41

Edwards Air Force Base, 79
Emergency landing, 28
Engel, Connie J., 76, 79–86

Federal Aviation Administration (FAA) 17, 19, 125, 128
  inspectors, 26–31, 64
  instructors, 26–31
  license exam, 17–30
Felder, N. Drue, 108–9
Felder, Tony D.A., 99–110
Field breaks, 129
Flight engineer, 15, 50, 64–65
Flight related skills, 19, 50
Flight schedules, 105–7 (chart)
Flight schools
  commercial, 57–65
  military, 32–45
  private, 17–31
Flight simulator, 61–63
Frontier Airlines, 71, 73, 74

Go-around, 29
Gravity, 20
  G-forces, 40, 62
Ground school, 20–22

Harbula, Gene, 78

Helicopter pilots, 41–42
High work, 28
Hypersonic transport (HST), 135

Johnson, Lyndon B., 121
Jones, Claudia, 67–71

Kennedy, John F., 121

LaSauce, Kathy, 78–79, 84
Laughlin Air Force Base, 33
Lindbergh, Charles A., 102
Link Trainers, 114
Livingston, Mary M., 84

Management pilot, 130
Military flight training
  Air Force, 13–15, 32–45
  Army, 41–42
  Navy, 41–42, 99–101
Mills Field. *See* San Francisco International Airport.
Moody, Douglas, 111–23, 136

National Aeronautics and Space Administration (NASA), 85
National Guard, 76
National Transporation Policy Study Commission, 132
Naval Reserve Officers' Training Corps, 114
Navigation, 34, 36, 37, 60
  radio, 23, 28
Navy
  air training program, 41–42, 101
Nixon, Richard M., 121

Oasis Aviation, Inc., 69

Pan American World Airways, 111, 115–21
Pentagon, 44
Pilot bidding, 105
Pilots
  commercial, 9–15, 46–51. *See also* Airline pilots.
  helicopter, 41–42
  military, 32–45. *See also* Air Force, Army, Navy.
  private, 17–31

144

INDEX

Radio navigation, 23, 28
Rambo, Kathleen A., 84
Randolph Air Force Base, 37, 79
Redundancy, 119
Reese Air Force Base, 33
Rogers, Susan D., 82–84, 85

San Francisco International Airport, 111
Sapp, Russell, 87–98, 102–3, 136
Scherer, Carol Ann, 84
Schott, Christine E., 84
Scott, Sandra May, 84
Spaulding, Richard L., 137
Spirit of St. Louis, The (film), 102
Spirit of St. Louis (plane), 112
Stalling, 20, 28

Stewart, Jimmy, 102
Strain, Larry, 19–31

Undergraduate Pilot Training (Air Force), 32–33
United Airlines, 114–16

Vance Air Force Base, 33
Visual flight rules, 19

Warner, Emily H., 71–74
Weather interpretation, 23
White House, 121
Williams Air Force Base, 33, 75
Women, 14–15, 44–45, 66–74, 75–86
Wright brothers, 66

The Author

Frank Stilley is the author of popular books from Putnam's—*The Search: Our Quest for Intelligent Life in Outer Space; The $100,000 Rat; Here Is Your Career: Veterinarian.* For many years Stilley was a writer and editor for the Associated Press. He and his wife, Joy, an editor-writer for AP Newsfeatures, live in New York, where he is a public relations consultant.